The Forties
When We Were
Dreamers of Dreams

by

Ray Barron

Library of Congress Cataloging in Publication Data

Barron, Ray, 1924-
   The forties—when we were dreamers of dreams.

   Includes index.
   1. Barron, Ray, 1924-. 2. World War, 1939-1945—United States. 3. United States—Social life and customs—1945-1970. 4. Advertising—United States—History—20th century. 4. United States—Biography.
I. Title.
CT275.B464A3 1987   973-917'092'4 87-5193
ISBN 0-8283-1915-4 (cloth).

Branden Publishing Company

17 Station Street
PO Box 843 Brookline Village
Boston, MA 02147-0843

Table of Contents

Dedicated

To my wife Marilyn
and daughters Karen and Robyn, who,
for many years
have coped with my dreamy-dreams.

Acknowledgements

Thanks to Adolpho, my editor for his encouragement and guidance.

Special thanks to the Advertising Club of Greater Boston for allowing me to sift through their archives.

John Cronin, *Boston Herald* librarian, my thanks for allowing me to pour over the countless files of the forties.

Without Nancy Ingersoll my words would never have found their way here.

There are many others I am indebted to for their encouragement, knowledge, time and patience.

The Forties
When We Were
Dreamers of Dreams
By

Ray Barron

Introduction

I wasn't around during the 40s. My mother was in Canada and my father in the military. It would be another decade before they would meet, marry and raise a family in Boston.

Growing up, as many boys did, I became fascinated by the history of World War II. My brother and I collected vast armies of toy soldiers and would fight to control North Africa, Italy and Germany (in his bedroom, in the hallway or in my bedroom, respectively).

During high school and college, I learned its fashion (splashy ties and wide lapels), the people (FDR and Truman), and the music (Glenn Miller).

Yet, thinking about the 40s is like opening an old scrap book. My mind brings forth snap shots, fragmented images like that of Betty Grable's legs, Churchill flashing the V sign, FDR arriving at Warm Springs, a sailor kissing his girl on VJ Day, the mushroom cloud over Hiroshima, and many others. But these snap shots are in black and white. They are still, lifeless images in time and place.

Ray Barron has given them color. He's brought these images back to life, and made them live and breathe, speak and dream for us.

He's made the 40s as real as the 80s, the decade in which I write this introduction.

From D-Day and the liberation of Europe, to the big bands, to the growth of the advertising industry, Ray gives an intimate portrait of a decade whose people *dared* to dream again after years of depression and of war.

But it's not just what he does—many books have been written about this period. It's how he does it. The book is a unique mixture of personal memoirs filled with adventure novel and historical essays.

My purpose is to introduce you to the work and to the author. Having done the former, now let me tackle the latter.

I've had the pleasure of knowing Ray Barron personally and professionally for a number of years. Because he is such a character, people who do not know him as well as I do often ask me: "What is Ray Barron really like?" What they mean is: did he really do everything he says he did? Is he really as exciting and outspoken as he seems to be?

Well, what are any of us really like? Aren't we all part truth and part myth? So, when I get this question, I simply smile and say: "One thing about Ray, he's never boring!"

That's also true of that decade and of this book. So, if you were around in the 40s, you'll feel the thrill of returning memories. If you weren't around, you'll feel the thrill of discovery—both sensations priceless!

Capel States

Towards the middle of my life,
I found myself astray in a dark forest
And the right path nowhere in sight.
The Divine Comedy
Dante Alighieri

Prologue

The quote of Dante seemed particularly apropos for nearly every American during the Depression years. Certainly, it was for me. Only a youngster (hardly midway through my life's journey), but I have keen recollections of the hardships of the Great Depression: the long lines at the employment office and welfare agencies, people down on their luck, few laughs, everybody looking grim. In spite of those burdens heaped upon us during that cruel period, family units seemed closer. In my case, it was no different—perhaps, a bit more heightened.

With my father dying when I was four years old, my mother was left with four small children to care for. As a result, we were forced to go on welfare.

With the dawning of a new era—the 40s—the Great Depression was finally becoming a bad dream. More Americans were working and beginning to enjoy steady income. As a result, young and old became dreamers of dreams, believing that prosperity and a better way of life were at hand. It was, indeed, time to look ahead.

Then, we all found out differently. The 40s would not be the golden era, but a decade filled with darkness and horror, pain and death. America, and the rest of free world, would be faced with its sternest test in history: World War II.

There was a clear danger that we might all become enslaved to Fascism (better known as Nazism), sweeping across Europe. And the things we held dear in our Democracy—freedom of speech, freedom to disagree, freedom to travel as we pleased, and many more freedoms—teetered on the brink of collapse.

While World War I was billed as "the war to end all wars", the second war provided the greatest challenge. Weaponry had advanced to a frightening stage, and the war in itself would culminate with man's most awesome weapon—the atomic bomb.

Without a doubt World War II was America's mightiest test in history. The fact that we ultimately triumphed signaled a turning point in our history, a period we can look back upon and realize that things could never be the same again.

Certainly, they weren't for me. Thanks to the 40s, my life would never be the same. That's what this book is about: the 40s—as a turning point in both my personal life—as a musician and art lover, and in my professional life—as a media specialist and advertising executive.

From a feature article to a book.

Chapter One

On a recent cold evening, sitting at the piano at home, I found myself playing music from the 30s and 40s—mostly Cole Porter tunes.

While playing, I began to think about life during those years—the years of growing up, when I entered manhood. Suddenly, I thought about how people, working in advertising, survived during the depression and the decade of the 40s. I stopped playing and went to my writing table.

"The Advertising Industry During World War II" was the title of the short piece I had intended to do for a column in the *Boston Herald*, or for the *New England Ad Week*. It would be interesting to research the war years, and speak with individuals affiliated with agencies and broadcasting during those years.

What was to be a short piece began to grow. Soon, I began spending long hours at the Boston Public Library and at the *Boston Herald* pouring over files. I telephoned individuals in the field and began to get unusually interesting stories which helped me better understand this field of broadcasting and advertising, but thought their stories would also be of interest to others as well. Realizing this, I found myself plunging deeper and deeper into the subject. I interviewed people in-person, prompting them to recall their life and times. Some, well into their eighties, rolled back the decades and told their stories of struggle and success, convincing me that I had made the right choice on entering the business of broadcasting and advertising. It was thrilling to sit and listen to people who actually laid the groundwork, who molded and shaped the future of the ad business for those of us following in their footsteps. Thanks to their input, what began as a feature article was turning into this book—for which I am grateful. This experience has been thoroughly enjoyable.

Because of the war, many working in advertising were forced to take on more responsibilities. The draft, of course, deeply affected the industry. Young men, who had just begun their careers, were called up for military service, interrupting many a career. The growing shortage of personnel added more work for those left behind.

These people brought respectability to our profession. It was in the 40s that advertising, often maligned as a huckster's domain, began to find itself. The men and women working in advertising and in the broadcasting end pioneered the industry for those of us yet to launch our careers.

Years later—in 1965—Samuel Eliot Morrison, the distinguished Bostonian author and historian, said that advertising, more than any factor, has made the luxuries of yesterday the necessities of today. If any profession is to be crowned or cursed for bringing about the present state of society, it is that of the *ad man*.

Crowned or cursed! Ad people are crowned when their advertising produces results for their clients, cursed when their campaigns fail to show anything.

Certainly, advertising reached its crowning glory during the years when it was mobilized to help the war effort. Billboards, newspapers, magazines and radio stations urged the public to join in a united effort to sell war bonds, ration gas and meat, save on electricity and heat, and to turn in tin cans for recycling, among other things.

After the war, as the decade came to a close, a turning point entered the lives of most Americans. Returning soldiers took advantage of veterans benefits. Some, never believing it possible, went on to college or enrolled in trade schools; others made use of VA home mortgage loans, thus creating a veritable housing boom.

There was a growing consumer market for products once rationed during the war. For anyone fortunate enough to have a job and a steady income, a brand new Cadillac was available for $5,000, a gabardine suit for $50, a 10-inch table television for $250. Cigarettes sold for 21 cents a pack, a pound of pork cost 57 cents, and a bottle of Coca Cola was only a nickel. Those were the days!

Many of us did face an uncertain future. At that time, a career in advertising had never entered my mind. With the aid of the GI Bill, I was able to further my education, eventually carving out a career in advertising.

My first job was with the Mina Lee Simon Agency, which played an important role in my career. As an advertising copywriter, I earned the kingly sum of $50 per week. My copy chiefs were Alice Kaplan and Cecil Landau, who became my "guiding light and mentor".

The Mina Lee Simon Agency was the only full-service agency operated by a woman in Boston, located on Tremont Street.

It is interesting to note that most of the ad agencies in the Boston area were owned by Yankees and the Irish, with only a small percentage owned by Jews.

But I'm jumping way ahead of myself. To tell it properly, I have to turn back the clock to when it all started—in the Italian neighborhood of East Boston.

Chapter Two

I've been billed by the Associated Press as being "outrageous!" I don't know how that came about.

A more elaborate portrayal appeared in the *East Boston Times-Leader-Free Press* on June 26, 1985, wherein I was characterized as having a "reputation of infuriating his advertising and media colleagues with his keen wit and enjoys his capacity to shock even the most vainglorious and outspoken person with his forthright and self-prophetic manner.

"The man described, however, is only a mere reflection of his exterior self; an outward style that can easily be misconstrued, upon a first impression, as being characteristic of his total personality. It is true that his speeches at the many colleges, high schools, trade and social organizations and his columns in the *Boston Herald* and *New England Ad Week* convey this aspect of his identity. His wit is at times caustic, but it is tempered by his ability to make fun of himself in proclaiming himself 'the man with the pear-shaped body.' However, upon a closer look, this highly successful and energetic man is an extremely sensitive complex person with a genuine concern for people."

I was pretty happy about the piece, but also a bit red-faced and embarrassed. I've always had a problem accepting kudos, especially when they're in print. Suddenly, you become glaringly exposed—whether it be true or not!

As for the truth, I was born Joseph Barisano on Everett Street in East Boston, a crowded neighborhood of myriad triple deckers inhabited mostly by Italian families. Conditions were harsh, particularly in the wintertime when people huddled around coal stoves in cold water flats in order to keep warm.

In our house, my mother would have us sit by the black stove in the kitchen all bundled up. She would tell us stories about her girlhood years in the old country, about the time when she was eight and was entrusted with the chore of feeding the chickens and finding herself, the following year, already baking bread for the entire family.

"We all had to work," she said. "If we didn't, we would have nothing to eat. My father and brothers used to work hard from early morning to late at night. There was always something to do when you live on a farm and have animals."

She would also relate mystery stories from that far away land that was once her home. One such story dealt with a ghost that kept chasing her in the evenings while returning home via a pathway. "It must have been a ghost!" she exclaimed in hushed tones, while we listened, both fascinated and fearful. "It was a long, flowing white outline that came after me as I was walking the path to my home. We didn't have street lights like here in America, and that white ghost chased me, and I ran as fast as I could until I reached the safety of the house."

Recalling that story, I think she may have been trying to tell us to stay home.

My mother possessed a wonderful imagination, and you can guess how much we looked forward to her ghost stories on those cold and wintry nights as we sat around the stove, enjoying hot thick slices of Italian bread she had baked.

She never failed to remind us that in Mirabella (a little town where they have the beautiful feast of the Straw Obelisk), it was never as cold as it was in East Boston. "We only had a little snow once or twice in ten years," she commented. My sister Fannie would ask her if she wished to be back there, but my mother never admitted any desire to return to the farm in Passo

Eclano, a suburb of Mirabella. Years later, I sort of put the pieces together as to why she preferred the cramped East Boston neighborhood over the wide-open country environment of Eclano. In a nutshell, it boiled down to one word: hope. Although we didn't have much, at least there was the hope that someday things would change for the better, while in Eclano, conditions were rather mean (they didn't have a bathroom, for example, and had to use the stable under the house), and there was little hope for any future improvement. Having visited the place recently, I am happy to tell that things have changed for the better, in some instances very drastically. I guess, there is hope there too!

I don't remember much about my father. He died at the age of 29, when I was only four years old. My mother, then 25, was left with four small children—my three sisters and me—and was forced to go on welfare. We barely survived. Most of our meals consisted of pasta and thick crusty Italian bread, and we wore second-hand clothes. When I started school, my mother secured a coat with safety pins, as there were no buttons. I often complained about the pins. "Mama! How am I going to take this coat off? I'll never get out of this thing."

When there was snow on the ground, she insisted on putting galoshes on my feet. I hated them! I'd argue that there wasn't much snow on the ground and no need for galoshes, but she'd grab me by the shoulders and shake me. "Shut up! It's cold and there's a lot of snow. You'll only get your shoes wet and I can't afford to buy you another pair. So, shut up!"

At school, I always had difficulty getting the galoshes off, and would hate my mother for making me wear them. Getting home for lunch, she would notice that I hadn't pinned my coat together, and scold me: "Do you want to freeze to death? Stupid! Is that what you want? What am I going to do with you?"

So, I'd prepare for a pinch you know where or a slap across the face. Then she would order me to sit down and eat. Eat! Eat what? Lunch usually consisted of a bowl of hot cocoa and stale bread which we'd break into pieces and soak in the hot bowl of cocoa.

My mother was a very loving and gentle woman. One of my fondest memories goes back to Christmas Day 1929. I was only five, and the year before she had promised me that if she ever had the money she would buy me a toy drum. I had gotten the idea for the drum on seeing a funeral procession come by our house. Marching behind the hearse was a band playing a mournful piece. My eyes caught the drummer with his sticks lightly hitting the skin of the drum, accentuating the rhythm of the music. I liked that sound so much that afterwards I begged my mother to buy me a toy one. That gift was to have had a great impact on my later career in music.

On Christmas, I still remember, I discovered the gift on the floor behind the black coal burning stove where I had hung the stocking. The happiest kid in the world! I practiced on that little drum for hours each day. I was 14 years old when I finally bought a real set of drums and quickly organized a band with some of my English High School chums. It was at this time that I decided to change my name to Ray Barron.

I got it from my last name, Barisano. Barron sounded more professional for a band leader's name. Originally, it was to be Baron (with one r), but because it was misspelled by the *printer* on my business card, I decided to keep it anyway. As for changing my first name, I took it from a kid in the band named Ray—a name I liked a lot. I don't know why, but I'm not sure that the other Ray liked the idea.

My youthful activities weren't just focused on music. I was also impressed by the power of the press. While other kids dreamed of becoming fire fighters or Canadian Mounted Policemen, I wanted to become a reporter and see my name over a story.

My first venture into journalism occurred at the age of 12 when I launched a two-page newspaper using an antique hand-press. Called *The Tattletale*, it survived for three weeks. (I still have a copy). Soon after, I discovered another avenue that lead me to a career in journalism.

Back then, there was a radio program sponsored by Ward Bond Bread, which used news items submitted by kids. To be an authorized "Scoop" Ward Bond Bread reporter, I sent for a press card. You can imagine the thrill on receiving mine. It made me a reporter!

Joining me on the trail for the big news stories was this tall, stringy kid, Jimmy Geggis, who later went on to great fame as a reporter for the Associated Press and WHDH-TV. One of his biggest stories was his covering the sinking of the *Andrea Doria*, the luxury liner that sank off of our coast, for which he won a coveted award.

Anyway, as soon as Jimmy and I received our "Scoop" Ward Bond Bread reporter credentials, we took off in search of real life drama stories, by beginning to cover the frozen-over beach on Bayswater Road in East Boston, looking for kids on the ice floats, hoping one would fall into the freezing waters causing us to plunge in for the rescue (I guess you'd call that participatory reporting), and receive national acclaim for our heroic deed, with a by-line story written by us on how it happened.

Well, it didn't quite turn out that way. On a bitter cold Saturday morning, the beach was deserted, except for a few crazy seagulls crying over our heads, looking for food I guess. There were no kids anywhere hopping over the ice floats, though we kept on scanning the ice water for hours. Finally, after submitting ourselves to frost bites—deciding that discretion was the better part of valor (besides, our . . . were freezing off)—we finally went home to warm up. The hell with national acclaim!

When my mother remarried, we moved to Orient Heights, a predominantly Irish neighborhood and new friends. No Rocco, Antonio, or Carmine here, but Elmore, Lamplough, Hennigan, Aylward—forget it!

Henry Hennigan eventually made his living in the world of journalism as a typesetter and later in advertising sales at the Lynn Item.

On Friday morning of June 24, 1938, I officially graduated from Blackington School in the Orient Heights section of East Boston. I have vivid memories of that morning because of my clowning around during rehearsal. For punishment, the principal made me sit with the girls! My dear mother, who was in attendance, for some reason never questioned why I was the only boy on stage seated with the girls. I'm glad for that, because I don't think I could have devised a ready excuse.

The graduation edition of *The Blackington School Crier* magazine profiled the members of the class of 1938 for our life's ambitions. "To be a businessman" was my answer, and also listed the following activities: secretary of the Debating Club, 1st Lieutenant of our cadet company. Yes, it was mandatory in the Boston school system for junior and high school boys to practice "drilling" once a week. At the Blackington School, we marched around the schoolyard to the chant of, "left, right, left, right. . .to the rear, march!" and all of that. It was sort of like a forerunner to "popular-unpopular" ROTC of today—popular when threatened, unpopular when living off the fat of land?

Because of Miss Ryan, an attractive young, blonde teacher who was club supervisor, I joined the school's Debating Club. She was my seventh grade home room teacher and I had such a crush on her—to this day! I remember the boys raving about her legs. Oh, how many times we made our way to the waste paper basket by her desk with crumbled balls of paper, kind-a bending down and peeking at her legs while depositing the paper.

In our year book, Eddie Corsetti listed his life's ambition to be a civil engineer. Never achieving that goal, he became a highly respected journalist and crime reporter for the *Boston Record-American* and later for the Boston Herald American.

Eugene Del Bianco, not in our graduating class, nevertheless wrote a poem honoring us, "On To Victory" which was included in the Blackington Crier graduation edition. Years later, he ended up in the advertising business at Arnold & Company and Harold Cabot & Company as an account executive and media buyer.

While a freshman (1939) at Boston English High School, I discovered *Down Beat* magazine, then published twice monthly. I gave more attention to each issue than to *Ivanhoe* or *Silas Marner*. Had there been a course "Big Bands and Musicians" I surely would have taken it and topped the class! Whatever I read in the magazine stuck with me. This knowledge of what was happening in the world of music also proved helpful during my military service. In many discussions about big bands, I would be asked to verify the stuff. "Didn't Harry James play for Benny Goodman?" "Who recorded *Three Little Sisters?*" The questions would be pumped at me. Naturally, I got a big kick out of providing answers that gained me stature—I mean prestige!

During my sophomore years, my homeroom class elected me as athletic captain, responsible for promoting athletic events, selling buttons imprinted with "EHS". Mr. William Ohrenburg, my homeroom teacher and football coach, made me an assistant manager of the football team, thus having to attend the practice sessions as well as all the football games at

Billings Field in West Roxbury. My duties? Tightening or replacing cleats and carrying water buckets to the *heroes* on the field—a water boy! Nevertheless, I enjoyed every minute of it, especially attending the games and sitting on the bench watching the contest raging on the field.

The following year, however, with my report card grades tumbling, I was forced to curtail these activities. When I told Mr. Oherenburg I could no longer continue, he retorted by calling me a quitter—in front of my classmates. I'll never forget it: I was devastated!

I was no quitter and I knew it. But there was nothing I could do to defend myself. As bad as the incident was, it helped shape my life. It made me try harder to succeed. No matter what I set out to do, I was determined to always give it my best shot.

1940—The year before all hell broke loose.

Chapter Three

Here's a headline that will never be used again: "Gay Crowds Hail New Year". Guaranteed!

It appeared in the *Boston Herald* in 1940, a year in which "gay" had a totally different connotation. The story read: "With a hurricane of enthusiasm and a flood of wassail, the old year scurried out and the new took a bow as more than a million celebrators made their night a jubilant one in Boston's streets, theaters, hotels, cafes, and night clubs, raising such an ear-splitting din that staid old Dame Boston must have clapped her hands to her ears in dismay. Pent up slightly—but only slightly—by Sunday laws in the dime and dance places, hilarity let go with a tumult at midnight when dancing became legal and all lids were off. The fact that liquor selling was outlawed only 60 minutes later did not wreck the merry-making, for the storm of festivities was still roaring along at highest velocity when 3 o'clock boomed."

That was some piece of writing! It really captured the spirit of Boston back then. The demons of the 30s and of the Great Depression were exorcised for good. The only foreboding hint of future menace was in another front page story: "Meanwhile, in Berlin, the war's first New Year arrived in Germany in a complete blackout. . ."

We were not at war as was Germany, but ominous clouds were hovering over Europe. Who knew they'd be coming over.

Newspaper ads in 1940 prompted a bed sheet sale at Filene's for 89 cents. At Gilchrist's, fur trimmed coats sold for $28, and Jordan Marsh offered hand-tailored ties for $1.00.

At Loew's Orpheum, *Gone With the Wind* was being held over for a record third week, while Charles Laughton was starring in *The Hunchback of Notre Dame* at Keith Memorial.

At the Latin Quarter on Winchester Street, an ad inveigled the public to come see *La Conga Revue* featuring "Glamorous Cuban Girls" "Hot from Cuba". Along with the show, there was a "Delicious Dinner" for $1.50.

Speaking of which, this charming story appeared in the *Boston Traveler* entitled, "Leap Year Parties are Suggested":

"Here's your chance girls! Get your man with a leap and a bound. You've probably been reminded for the past month that 1940 is a leap year, so leap right in and make the most of your opportunity. We've planned your party and each girl is assigned a man to escort to the party, and must call for him. Throughout the evening, she must be attentive to him, the men aren't to dance unless the girls ask them to."

Gee, whatever happened to those leap year parties?

On a sour note, for all you Boston College fans, New Year's Day 1940 was a real downer. B.C. played Clemson in the Cotton Bowl classic in Dallas and lost the heartbreaker six to three.

And talk about how things have changed. The National Hockey League had only seven teams: the League leading Bruins, Toronto, New York Rangers, Montreal, Chicago, New York Americans and Detroit. Enough about sports.

Having survived the turbulent 30s, the world of advertising was growing stronger. In spite of the mass unemployment during the Depression, many companies continued to advertise their products and services. While newspapers and magazines attracted most of the budgets, suddenly advertising discovered that radio reached more people—all at the same time. Radio became so powerful and influential that it inspired President Franklin Delano Roosevelt to address the nation with the first "Fireside Chats". As Americans glued themselves to the radio, advertising agencies began to create more inventive programs.

While people began to sense the availability of such luxuries as automobiles, war clouds began to appear. Advertising agencies, finally showing signs of prosperity, were again faced with uncertainties. If America went to war, how would it affect business? With shortages of products, would clients advertise?

There were other concerns. Some reports said that "advertising was biased" even "downright deceptive". Agencies came under fire, too. A story read: "One of the first principles of an advertising agency seems to be to minimize information and maximize emotional appeal."

A. H. Fairbanks, in an article published in *Printer's Ink*, stated: "Advertising to intelligence is passe. College professor logic and 100 percent truthful advertising do not pay."

Throughout the years, I've been buying out-of-print books about advertising at book sales or flea markets. My collection includes books published in 1910, 1920, 1924, 1927, and at least six published during the 30s. One of my favorites is *Advertising Copy* by George D. Hotchkiss and published in 1929. Another is *What About Advertising?* by Kenneth M. Goode and Harford Powell Jr., published in 1927. The authors included a statement on advertising by Edward S. Jordan, a well-known advertising executive during the 20s: "The trouble with advertising," he suggested, "is that there are too many clever people connected with the business, trying to make it complicated, instead of trying to make it simple."

Yes, advertisers and ad agencies were looked upon in a very negative way because of a lack of restraints on the part of advertisers. Until March 21, 1938, there were no legal restraints to keep us honest. On that date, the Pure Food and Drug Law was written, giving the Federal Government authority to prevent or punish interstate shipment of foods and drugs whose labels contained false or misleading statements. As a result, advertisers and their agencies became more cautious, causing advertising to grow up. It was the end of the era when Lucky Strikes used the slogan: "Reach for a Lucky instead of a sweet." Many future advertisers launched their products in 1940. Morton Packing Company was founded at Louisville, Kentucky, introducing its line of frozen foods, such as chicken, turkey and beef pot pies. M & M Candies began producing coated chocolates. Paul Dean Arnold and his wife, Betty, discovered an old brick oven lined with English tiles and began to bake bread with a distinctive taste which became known as Arnold Bread.

In 1940, the Junior Ad Club of Boston—the kiddies of the advertising industry—published a mimeographed newsletter the *Jr. Ad Lib* filled with gossip and tidbits. For example, Russ Mahan, chairman of membership, was praised for how he handled his duties. "Russ Mahan's cracking down on membership requirements scared several members away who couldn't qualify. Good work, Russ." But wait! Later in the piece he was referred to as the club's "official bouncer"!

One of the club's restrictions was that a potential member had to be under 29 in order to qualify. Once you reached 29 years of age, you were eleigible to become a member of the Ad Club. Ironically, the Junior Ad Club, from what I learned, had a lot of fun and attracted lively guest speakers for their weekly meetings. The sessions were chaired by Bert Allen, who often came down hard on the kiddies by demanding they pay strict attention to the speakers.

"Do not disturb or interrupt them by talking or other noise," Bert would admonish the gathering. "Remember it is very hard for an inexperienced speaker to talk to an unappreciative audience. So, let's be a little more quiet and help the speaker." After one of these warnings, Bert would then introduce the next speaker, who turned out to be Tony Cucchiara—hardly an inexperienced speaker! The articulate Cucchiara proved to be highly informative and inspiring. Some of the kiddies attending the 1940 meeting are today's senior citizens who still recall Tony's talk about what it takes to become a good account executive.

By the way, Tony was then working as an account executive at Whitten Advertising on Tremont Street. He was the only Italian-American serving as an officer of the Junior Ad Club. A few years later, young Cucchiara launched his own agency, Copley Advertising.

Myron Silton was also an active member of the Junior Ad Club in 1940, the only Jewish member of the staff that published the club's newsletter. Years later, together with his brothers Ray and Jayson, Myron would launch their own advertising agency.

As Boston's advertising community enjoyed weekly luncheons featuring guest speakers, I was struggling through Spanish—mind you, not Italian (that I could have used), commercial law, English and chemistry at Boston English High. After school, wrapping up my homework, I would go to the clubroom in the basement to practice on my drums. (I must note that my mother had married again, this time a man of means, and we owned our house and even—a car! in the Orient Heights section of East Boston.)

In those days, playrooms were known as clubrooms. Sitting on a drum stool, I fantasized being a drummer for Tommy Dorsey or Glenn Miller.

By this time, I had formed my own band, and played for weddings or at social clubs. I hustled engagement notices in the *Boston Post*, calling the bride-to-be and asking if she was interested in hiring my band for the reception. I also used preprinted postal cards promoting *Ray Barron and His Orchestra*.

The majority of the bookings for weddings were for three or four pieces. I used to charge $7 a head, plus double for the band leader. Wages then averaged $2000 a year. Thirty-five bucks a week was considered good money. On some weekends, we had Saturday and Sunday bookings—windfalls for kid musicians. Where else could you earn $14 for six hours? The more I earned from playing gigs, the more I would invest into music arrangements or in new dark blue gabardine suits. Those were exciting times. . .the sky was the limit and we all envisioned making it on the bigtime circuit.

1941—War clouds gather.

Chapter Four

Boston held no limits on celebrating the New Year—1941, as over a million people crowded into the city to proclaim a boisterous welcome. "Frenzied with noise and vivid with lights, a Boston in which, under a blackout enjoyed an earthquake of New Year's Eve celebration last night. There were a million in the streets. . .", read the *Boston Herald* story.

But a grim headline over another story on page one observed soberly: "Hitler Promises Germany Complete Victory in 1941".

On the first day of 1941, Gilchrist's celebrated its 99th anniversary, while Jordan Marsh was enjoying its 90th year in business.

Later that day, Bostonians reveled in another way: Boston College beat Tennessee in the Sugar Bowl, 19 to 13, the victory being capped by Charley O'Rourke's famous touchdown run with time expiring.

In early 1941, some of Boston's major newspaper advertisers were, of course, retailers: Jordan Marsh, Filene's, Raymond's, R. H. White's, Conrad's and Gilchrist's. Interesting to note, beer companies were also consistent advertisers. Narragansett's ads featured cartoon by a not yet famous Dr. Seuss. Another brewery, Harvard Beer, promoted "export beer". One of the largest retailers of liquor, Hayward Wine and Liquor with two locations in downtown Boston, ran large space ads promoting a case of Samoset Ale for 75 cents. McKibben's Irish Whiskey was going for $2.49 a quart, whereas a London Dry Gin was advertised at 99 cents a quart.

There were 23 companies in Boston specializing in advertising displays, the largest being Federal Studios on Chardon Street, noted for window, counter and itinerant displays.

The active direct small houses were: Dickie-Raymond, John G. McDonald Company, and the F. S. Root Company launched in 1909.

Outdoor advertising companies were F. H. Birch, C.I. Brink, John Donnelly & Sons, and Eagle Advertising headed by Joe Cifre and Joe Commerford. Donnelly used the slogan, "The Donnelly Way", and ran billboards in Rhode Island, New Hampshire and Vermont, as well as in Boston. All of these outdoor companies would contribute in a big way during the war.

Many ads appearing in the papers were small space advertisers, such as Carter's Little Liver Pills, which promised to "wake up your liver bile—you'll jump out of bed in the morning rarin' to go."

Another small space advertiser, Lovalon Hair Rinse, claimed its product would "rinse away shampoo films, tints the hair as it rinses." Lovalon also claimed it was a pure, odorless hair rinse. . .wonder whatever happened to Lovalon?

Reading movie ads provided a stimulating experience! On March 6, 1941, a new movie, "So Ends Our Night", opened at Boston's Loew's State Orpheum, with Frederick March, Margaret Sullivan and Frances Dee. The headline copy read: "Theirs was a Dangerous Romance—An Impossible Love!" Bold copy: "Yet with a coverage born of tender devotion they dared life. . .danger. . .everything to make that love possible!"

We had two active radio production houses: Fidelity Recording and Kasper-Gordon Studios, creating musical jingles and spots for many of Boston's leading stores, including Filene's and Jordan's. Electronic transcriptions (large platters) were used to record the spots. And guess what? The platters were referred to as "E. T. 's." Just goes to show you there's nothing new under the sun.

Of the 83 advertising agencies, some are still active today: Harold Cabot, Doremus & Co., Ingalls (then known as Ingalls Miniter, and Daniel R. Sullivan & Co.)

Other notable firms were: BBD&O, N.W. Ayer, Harry Frost, Eddy-Rucker-Nickels, Badger & Browning, John C. Dowd, Frank Albert-Guenther Law, Sutherland-Abbot, and Chambers & Wiswell.

Interestingly, there were three public relations agencies: Carpenter Delphine, Harris-Mann Associates, and Stoddard Associates. We did have four publicity bureaus, however: Floyd Bell Associates, William Frany, Harriet O'Brien and Mary Armstrong Melvin.

Fay Foto, located at West Canton Street, specialized in commercial and "flashlight" photography. Many agencies did business with Fay Foto, and with Benjamin Morse, and Shaw Commercial Photographers.

The favorite meeting place for many working in advertising and allied industries was the Statler Hotel, now known as the Park Plaza. That was because the Ad Club of Boston held its Wednesday luncheons there and people in the business knew it was the place to go to catch up on the latest gossip in the industry, including news about individuals drafted into the armed forces.

Edwin Leason was the president of the Advertising Club of Boston, and John Nicodemus the following year. Ernest Hoftyzer of the *Boston Record-American* served as president from

1942 to 1943. In 1944, at the height of the war, Fred Bliss
succeeded Hoftyzer.

As the war was coming to an end, Paul Swaffield was elected
the club's chief executive. (For the record, Nicodemus,
Hoftyzer and Swaffield are all deceased). I had hoped to review
the Ad Club's membership list covering the war years, but no
records were available. Misplaced? Tossed out? ¿ *Quien sabe?*

This much I do know: it started out as a sexist organization
in 1904, its original name being, The Ad Men's Club of
Boston. Five years later, the founding fathers adopted the
name, The Pilgrim Publicity Association. Its members also
agreed to wear, at local gatherings as well as national conven-
tions, blue serge coats, white flannel trousers, white shoes, and
straw hats with a blue ribbon and the inscription "Pilgrim" on
it.

In 1924, another name change occurred, but not until after
some heated debate among members. It seems that the older
ones wanted to keep the same name but their argument was
defeated; thus a new name was born: The Advertising Club of
Boston.

On looking over the officers of the Pilgrim Publicity Association, I came to understand why some of the older members
were reluctant to change the name. They were old-line WASPS
(perhaps reluctantly) rubbing elbows with the upstart Irish.

As a way of illustrating attitudes of the members back then,
I am reprinting an "Early History of the Advertising Club of
Boston" by Tilton S. Bell. I am sure you will find it as enjoya-
ble and interesting as I did.

Early History of Advertising Club of Boston
by Tilton B. Bell

"At the beginning of the 20th Century, it was the custom for
many magazine representatives living in New York to visit

Boston advertisers and advertising agencies. A number of the boys came over here regularly—many of them being personal friends of the Boston representatives, and in the course of conversations the Boston boys were challenged to a baseball game by the New York boys—which challenge was only accepted and the time and place for the game selected.

"The owners of the old baseball grounds on Columbus Avenue offered the free use of their diamond for this historic event. It was intended that only those actually engaged in the buying and selling of advertising were eligible to play in this game but somehow or other through underground channels the Boston boys learned that the New York boys were going to bring over some well known college players, not particularly identified with the advertising profession. This set the Boston boys thinking and they decided to add to their strength by getting some well known players, particularly from Harvard and Dartmouth.

"The game was played and nobody to this day remembers who won, nor the score, but it was a most enjoyable event. After the game the players and a few of their friends adjourned to the Hotel Berkeley (located at that time on the corner of Berkeley and Boylston Streets) for the evening meal and general jollification and it was during this dinner that the suggestion was made that the Boston boys form an advertising club. This suggestion was adopted and the Ad Men's Club of Boston was born at that time—1904.

"It is interesting to note that, of the Boston boys who took part in this baseball game 37 years ago, Harold Barber, Charlie Bellatty, Walter Sampson, Billy Soule and Allen Wood are still active or connected with the advertising business. Tilton Bell, the Club's oldest living Ex-President, was among the spectators—which were composed mostly of Young America of the Roxbury neighborhood.

"The Club consisted of two officers—a President and a Secretary-President. Dues were nominal, just enough to cover the cost of printing, postage and mailing notices. Meetings were held whenever the spirit moved—whenever the President and Secretary could obtain a worthwhile speaker. Such meetings when held were usually at the Boston Yatch Club on Rowes Wharf.

"These meetings were very popular and successful— generally attended by a large congregation. The only Annual event was the Christmas Party at which a generous collection in cash was taken and presented to the Salvation Army, often amounting to over one hundred dollars.

"There were no by-laws, rules or regulations other than an unwritten law that the President of the Club should be an Advertising Representative—Advertising Agent or an Advertising Manager—and in this rotation as far as practicable.

"The Club proceeded along these lines for many years and continued with the same name until 1909 when at the urgent insistence of George B. Gallup the name was changed to the Pilgrim Publicity Association—which name continued through the big national convention in Boston in 1911.

"The old Ad Men's Club succeeded in bringing many notable speakers to Boston—President Taft—Senator Beverdige of Indiana—Mr. Post from Battle Creek, Michigan (originator of Post Toasties)— Mr. Brown of the Divine Press—U.S. Secret Service Head Burns—Elbert Hubbard—John Kendrick Bangs Gen. Charles H. Taylor—and others.

From 1904 to 1908 the Club existed simply as a good fellowship club, to dine together once in a while. In 1908 the first planned program was outlined and an effort made to have regular meetings on regular dates. This succeeded fairly well.

In 1909 the first annual Picnic of the Pilgrims was held at Nantasket Beach with several hundred members, their families and friends present. The Pilgrims were noted for their Convention attendance and at Toronto, Baltimore, Philadelphia and Dallas large delegations were present. The Pilgrims wore on such occasions a blue serge coat, white flannel trousers, white shoes, straw hats with a blue band inscribed PILGRIM and received a great deal of favorable attention and comment wherever they were. They paraded in company formation."

A World at war.

Chapter Five

On March 6, 1941, the *Boston Daily Record* carried the advertisement headline, "Keep U. S. A. Out of War". The ad was created and placed by The Peace House of New York, and urged the readers to write Massachusetts Senators David I. Walsh and H. Cabot Lodge Jr. to oppose a bill which would empower the president to cancel the Neutrality Act.

Such efforts were futile, in the end. On December 7, Japan bombed Pearl Harbor, and the U.S. was at war. Soon after, Congress extended military conscription to men between the ages of 20 to 44; on November 13, 1942, it was lowered to 18.

Summoned by the local draft board to register, I wasn't too concerned over being drafted, but I knew that sooner or later I would be called up. Only 17, I was totally immersed in my music career, hoping someday to establish the Ray Barron orchestra in attractive ballrooms.

Up to then, my only experience with advertising was a piece of literature to promote the band. It simply read, "Music for All Occasions".

The *orchestra* consisted of teenagers. As we began to mature, gasoline was rationed, thus restricting our travels. Individuals working in defense or government related employment were allowed to obtain special car stickers entitling them to extra gas. Undaunted, I found a way to get a sticker—legitimately, that is. Fresh out of high school, I took a job in defense work and got a sticker which I put on my stepfather's Oldsmobile I

used to get around to gigs. (If you can't fight them, join them!)
The defense job? That was in South Boston on C Street, where I
unloaded freight cars at a warehouse for the U. S. Army Signal
Corps. As a laborer, I was a disaster. The foreman, a burly
Irishman, repeatedly told me I was useless, that I goofed off too
much and talked incessantly. Well, I did talk a lot, to be
honest with you, mostly about music and my band, which he
didn't appreciate. My whole life was consumed by my passion
for music, and the defense job was only a means to an end:
getting a sticker for extra gas.

The job didn't last long. Uncle Sam, however, had other
ideas. On February 4, 1943, my draft board sent me to Boston
with a group of other 18-olds to take a physical. A week
later—February 11, my mother's birthday, I was off to Fort
Devens to serve in the Army—an experience I will never forget.
Suddenly, I was being transformed from a music-crazy teenager
into a *fighting machine?*—all at the same time.

The day I left home, The Ice Follies were appearing at
Boston Garden, while on-stage, at the RKO Boston, was Jan
Savitt and his band, plus the John Herley band. Given the
opportunity, I would have taken in the "battle of bands" at
RKO.

The big story was about the Germans evacuating Kharkov in
Russia as well as the British Eight Army rolling forward to
Tunisia, North Africa.

In Boston, the trial of Dr. Harry Sagansky of Brookline,
under indictment in Suffolk County on charges of operating a
huge number pool lottery, was the big story. Also in the news,
the aroma of goats was being debated in the Massachusetts
Senate after Senator Donald Nicholson of Wareham expressed
doubt as to the value of a bill providing for state inspection of
horse, mule and goat meat. "As for goats," he said, "if the meat
smells anything like the goat, I don't know why anybody

would want to eat it." Senator Charles Olson of Ashland defended the species: "I resent the remarks of the senator", he said. "Anybody who has kept goats knows that only the bucks smell—goats are clean."

I was on my way to Fort Devens, starting my first day in the Army; the problem of goat odors wasn't even remotely on my mind.

On my second day there, we learned that Rommel's Afrika Korps had launched a massive break through the Kasserine Pass, threatening to cut the Allied armies in two. We also learned that our GIs were taking a beating. As we sat around the barracks, we speculated about our future role in the army. Would we be shipped to North Africa after basic training? The next morning, at chow, we learned that General Patton and his armored divisions put a stop to Rommel's advancing Afrika Korps. This was great news! But, for some reason, I feared being shipped to North Africa.

At Devens we were issued new uniforms, instructed on how to make up our bunk beds, and briefed about "short arm" inspections. This caused many of us to blush, as the sergeant explained how to grasp our penis and work it for inspection by a medical officer. This was our first education about venereal diseases. For 18-year olds, it proved to be a shocker—the first of many. We learned another lesson—no more privacy. "You're in the Army now!"

Two weeks later, I was shipped to Camp Swift, Texas, serving with the 97th Infantry Division. After basic training, I was re-assigned to escorting and guarding German prisoners of war assigned to rubbish collection in the camp. I was handed a 12-gauge double barrel shotgun and instructed to use it only if the prisoners attempted to escape or attack me. Egads! I had never fired a shot gun and I was told it could knock you on your ass when you fired one! My "wards" were six Germans—a happy lot, sitting out the war in Texas. On occasions, they would break out singing songs. As a guard or "prison chaser", I was not allowed to get friendly with them, but they tried constantly to make friends with me by smiling or by showing me pictures of their mothers or wives (never their sisters or girlfriends).

At the camp dump, the prisoners would scavange for newspapers or magazines; more than once, I caught them trying to stuff the publication in their pants. I would yell, "No! No! No!" They understood. We were told not to let them read any materials. A week later, I let them take the newspapers and magazines back to the compound. Big mistake!

One day, I had a close call behind the quarter master supply depot building. One of them began to taunt me, which I interpreted as poking fun at me because I had to guard them. Since I didn't understand German, I sensed his remarks insulting as his comrades laughed loudly. I told him to knock it off. But he continued, and, at the same time, began to pretend he was going to attack me. On coming within range, I walloped him on the side of the head with the barrel of my shotgun, sending him stumbling to the ground. I began to swear my head off, warning all of them that if any of them made one more move, I'd blow their heads off! It worked.

On returning them to the compound, they immediately filed charges against me for an unwarranted attack. That evening, I was summoned to the commanding officer who gave me a royal ass chewing, telling me that, under the Geneva pact regarding prisoners of war, my actions might be interpreted as violating the law, that I could be court martialed and sentenced to prison. The Colonel, sensing my panic, told me I was dismissed, but to watch myself. I saluted him, turned, and quickly marched out the room, smartly. A sergeant told me later I probably was a marked man, adding that the Germans would have it in for me. Looking back on it, I'm sure he was only trying to scare me. At that time, I was easy to scare—to a point.

The next morning, I was told that I would be doing guard duty at another facility which turned out to be a WAC officers' barrack—all women! So I spent night after night walking around the barracks, occasionally talking to the women soldiers either leaving or reporting for work. After a week, I was transferred to standing guard at a small airplane landing strip, near the outskirts of the camp. The new assignment was a horror! Alone out in the middle of nowhere, standing in a wooden shack equipped with a field telephone wired directly to guard headquarters, pulling the midnight to four in the morning shift. The first hour wasn't too bad, since I walked around the area and sneaked a smoke in the little shack. A lot of things ran through my mind: home, music, women, food, friends, and how the war was going.

After exhausting myself with so many thoughts, I began to study the area—a mistake! I suddenly began to imagine escaped German prisoners hiding out there making sounds. I was actually (unwittingly) scaring myself to death! I did hear a sound off and on, but couldn't figure out where it came from or what it was. Panic set in! Germans? Bob cats? Jesus! I better call in for help. I cranked the phone until. . . "Sergeant of the guard!"

"Sarge, there's something around here, and I don't know what it is. I hear whirling sounds off and on. I think you had better send someone out here, fast. I don't think I can take any more of this. . ."

The sergeant said he'd send a couple of soldiers. While I waited, I sweated profusely—I was that scared. When the jeep finally arrived, two guys jumped out and asked me what I was hearing, and where it was coming from. I pointed ahead, and we all began walking to a barbed wire fence stretching between wooden posts. On getting closer, we suddenly heard the noise.

We were startled but only for an instant until we saw a small wooden propeller nailed to one of the posts, whirling around with the wind.

Soon after, I was delighted to hear I was being relieved from guard duty, and ordered back to the barracks. Once inside, the sergeant looked at me and called me a "yellow belly". Me, a yellow belly? I guess I was!

That night I fell off to sleep dreaming about being back home in my own bed.

While at Camp Swift, advertising was the farthest thing from my mind. But I was aware of certain brand names as being useful to store in my footlocker. Among the most popular items sold at the Post Exchange were Kiwi Shoe Polish and Mennen After Shave Lotion, also used as an effective way to kill jiggers and wood ticks we picked up out in the field.

Years later, I constantly heard, "Take ten!" as a musician. It meant, "Take a break!" But it reminded me of the army. Many a time at Camp Swift, I used to look forward to hearing the sergeant shout, "Take ten!" as we dogged for ten miles wearing full field packs. On one extremely hot day, I didn't have the strength to wait for the ten minute break, having collapsed from exhaustion, and joining two others who had also given up—one a second lieutenant. It would not be the first time for many of us to hit the ground that way.

"Take ten!" was commonly used by orchestra leaders to signify it was time for the musicians to give their chops a rest. During the break, most musicians walk off either to one side or to the backside of the bandstand for a smoke. If you were playing with a small group for a wedding, "take ten" could result in prodding from members of the wedding party to keep playing. It's no wonder that wedding gigs often wore us out! The only rest we got was if the wedding reception was held at a

neighborhood hall and the food was served downstairs. Sometimes the musicians would be invited to join the reception,
seating us alone in the corner. I have lost track of how many
weddings we did. Some of receptions turned into brawls while
others turned into real posh affairs.

But, it's time to "take ten" in this tale. I'm getting ahead of
myself, again. In the next chapter, I'll take a look at advertising
in Boston before returning to my life in the army.

In 1941, the Advertising Club of Boston acted as host of the
Advertising Federation of America held in Boston from May 25
to 29. This marked the third time in thirty years the Ad Club
of Boston acted as host for the AFA. The conventioneers were
welcomed to Boston by Edwin Leason, president of the Advertising Club of Boston. The stately looking Leason reminded the
visitors in 1911, in Boston, the seed of the Truth-In-Advertis-
ing movement was germinated. And he went on to say, "In
1941 we meet again in Boston, in times that are troublous, in
the midst of grave uncertainties for advertising and for the
whole world. We take as our theme a slogan that is at once a
declaration and a challenge: 'Advertising—Its Service To Democracy Today.'"

Leason also offered the conventioneers to Boston an outline of
some of the planned activities during their stay such as an
exhibit of the new tools which suppliers have developed for use
in advertising, guest speakers and discussion forums. The
stately looking and articulate Edwin Leason then went on to
instill a sense of patriotism to the gathering: "It is particularly
fitting that a convention based on the services of advertising to
democracy should be held in Boston. For it was here that the
first strings of democracy were felt in the colonies. It was here
that the founding fathers of the Pilgrim colony drew up their
own laws and their own charter—the first declaration of free
men in the New World. And when that freedom was

threatened, it was from Boston that Paul Revere started on his famous ride to warn the farmers of the countryside.

"Before, in between, and after the business sessions, you will have time to visit some of the places in Boston that are hallowed by memories of our own fight for freedom. You can stand where men who chartered the course of the young nation once stood. You can visit shrines where every shadow whispers of great deeds and recalls tales of men who were determined that this nation should be a free, undivided nation, pledged only to itself. What better foundation can you have for your efforts to serve democracy through advertising?"

The applause was so long and loud! Leason's speech was timely and many a visitor left Boston proud to be a part of the advertising industry and its service to democracy.

"Advertising nourishes the consuming power of men. . .
It spurs individual exertion and greater production."

Sir Winston Churchill

Chapter Six

During February 1942, Boston's advertising community had the opportunity to attend weekly luncheons on Wednesdays at the Statler Hotel, now the Park Plaza. Some of the guest speakers included Lester Hawes, president of L. B. Hawes Advertising, recruited by Hoftyzer, advertising director of the *Boston Record-American*. Hawes delivered a case history about a cigar advertiser, explaining in great detail how he spent his limited advertising budget in newspapers and radio.

Another was Tim Dolan of the Research and Marketing Department of the Record-American. Tim, who had a good sense of humor, talked about his job and how he assisted in advertising campaigns for Noxema and Fels Napatha.

Betty Potter of "What's New in Town", a publication devoted exclusively to Boston life, spoke about her many and varied duties as assistant editor. She also told how she interviewed Raymond Scott, the band leader appearing at the Brunswick Hotel's Bermuda Terrace.

In 1942, Ernest Hoftyzer was president of the Ad Club.

What follows is his annual message to the members:
"PRESIDENT'S MESSAGE

This above all things:
To thine own self be true,
And it must follow, as the night the day,
Thou can'st not then be false to any man.
Hamlet

"We've seen many changes in this a year that has engulfed our nation in the holocaust of total war.

"We've seen our men leave to occupy far flung fronts in half a hundred different spots on the globe.

"We've paid the highest taxes in the history of our nation gladly, willingly and are prepared to pay more and more if necessary gladly and willingly.

"We've seen changes with a capital "C" and neophobia is a word we purposely choose not to understand.

"But in a world of turmoil and fear, in a discourant symphony of swift and sudden change, the Advertising club of Boston injects a constant and sustaining influence.

"Ever ready to sponsor the new idea, ever careful to guard the old custom, ever militant to defend the privileges synonymous with our American way of life. . .this, fellow members, has been the constant effort of our officers and directors for 1942-1943.

"Even greater than the knowledge that we have contributed so materially in stimulating a more intelligent interest in advertising and selling is the warm glow that comes to each and every one of us when we realize that more than one figure of national importance has lauded our club, first, for its downright patriotic endeavors and, second, for its advertising activities.

"For, the final analysis, the essence of any club's worth in any community is the measure in which its contributions serve in advancing the common good.

"It is our wish that the advancement of the common good continue to be the North Star of The Advertising Club of Boston."

With paper being rationed during the war, printers faced some trying times. Carter, Rice and Company. distributors of paper and located at 237 Summer Street, was making available to advertisers and ad agencies a series of booklets published by Oxford Paper Company such as, "Are You An Advertising Slacker?" or, "199 Ways To Sell Creative Printing In Wartime".

The Boston Globe, The Boston Post, and *The Boston Record-American* scheduled full-page ads in the 1942-43 Roll Call Issue of The Advertising News published by the Advertising Club of Boston. The *Globe* ad boasted "No other newspaper in American today is making a greater effort to bring to its readers the complete story of World War II." *The Boston Post* elected to prove how the paper's readers are responsive, explaining, "When the Army asked readers of all Boston newspapers to donate 1500 radios, *Post* readers swamped all the rest—1888 of them offered one or more radios each."

The Boston Record-American promoted the "new market" with a headline reading: "John Doe has become John Dough!" The body copy read: "The war had decidedly changed the condition of the skilled worker. After many lean years he has come into his own. Humming machinery, smoking smokestacks, ships, planes, tanks, guns, have poured unheard of wealth into his pockets. He is the new market—the buying market at which all advertising must strike. He is the basis for post war operations on which all advertising must build."

John Donnelly & Sons of Boston, the largest outdoor billboard company in New England, reminded the Boston advertising community of their public service in behalf of the government. Donnelly reported: "Today we carry a heavy

responsibility in behalf of our government. Our facilities have
been made available to government, and to civilian defense
groups in order that patriotic appeals may find powerful express
through outdoor advertising to help awaken the citizenry to the
need of the times."

It was during World War II when the *Boston Globe* began to
emphasize the importance of its Classified Advertising section,
which came at the urging of Andrew Dazzi. That section
proved one of the most profitable of the paper. In later years,
Dazzi was referred to as the "father of classified advertising".
Everyone knows what its Classified Section has meant to its
lifeblood. It is the heart, soul, and gristle of the paper—make
no mistake about it! The emphasis on classified advertising
proved to be the foundation upon which the *Globe* has built a
mighty newspaper, the biggest in New England.

Outdoor advertising, which originally experienced a drop in
billings due to the curtailment of automotive traffic, picked up
when the relaxation of these restrictions occurred.

In 1944, the War Advertisement Council created a series of
anti-venereal disease print ads as a "public service". When the
ads broke in newspapers and magazines, church leaders criti-
cized the campaign and pressured the Council to discontinue
the campaign, which they immediately did. But the anti-
venereal disease campaign was converted into film, in color,
and shown to newly drafted servicemen. It was a shocker!
When we saw on the big screen "the symptoms" of venereal
disease, many a young draftee fainted away.

Advertising agencies, which had as clients, makers of cigarettes, meat products, coffee, flour and canned goods (all rationed products), had to astutely plan their advertising.
Though many of the products were being rationed, advertising
continued in order to maintain their identity in the
marketplace.

As for brand loyalty during the war years, consumers settled on whatever was available. For example, they accepted any brand of cigarettes. As GIs, we found ourselves smoking a wide variety of them packed in our K-rations.

One new product introduced to war weary civilians that became the hottest selling item was the ballpoint pen. Gimbel's in New York promoted it with newspaper ads and a price of $12.50. It sold out in one day! One of the popular trade publications widely read by the advertising industry was *Advertising and Selling*. In 1943, it offered certificates for advertisements judged most meritorious for war service. These covered a wide range of advertisements, such as ads promoting the purchase of war bonds, observance of rationing rules, loyalty to work and reminders not to do too much "loose talking" about defense work and military movements.

In 1943, *Advertising Age* was selling for 10 cents a copy; an annual subscription cost $2.00. Some of the publication's big stories of the year were: "Army Bans Gift Mailing of Dailies and Magazines", "Time, Inc. Jumps Into Lead In Magazine Field", and "60,000,000 Cars Predicted For Postwar Period".

Also in 1943, three former Lord and Thomas advertising agency executives—Emerson Foote, Fairfax Cone and Don Belding—launched Foote, Cone and Belding in New York. Also launched in the same year was a new radio network, American Broadcasting Company (ABC), by *Life Savers* millionaire Edward Noble.

A year later, as we fought our way into France, Belgium, Holland and Germany, living off of K-rations and an occasional ration of powdered eggs, we used to dream of enjoying steaks and ice cream. Me, I dreamed of bananas. I hadn't seen one, let alone taste one, since leaving for England to prepare for "D" Day. Back home, bananas were being promoted as a brand name by United Fruit Company, using a massive radio advertising campaign with the jingle, "Chiquita Banana". Performed by the orchestra of Ray Bloch and vocalist Patti Clayton, the jingle became a hit song.

Another advertising campaign that captured wide attention was "Hunt for the Best", plugging Hunt Tomato Sauce and other Hunt products.

As the war was raging in Europe and in the Pacific, with many essentials being rationed, Americans, like the British, began to "dig for victory". It became known as the era of the Victory Garden, as millions began raising vegetables in their backyards.

Many leading food companies were urged by the government to package food for U. S. troops. Wrigley, noted for chewing gum, began preparing K-rations for combat troops. Packed inside the rations were compressed graham biscuits, small tin of canned meat, three tablets of sugar, four cigarettes, and a stick of chewing gum. There were also breakfast K-rations which, for the record, became my favorite. Included in the package was a small fruit bar and a packet of instant coffee developed by Maxwell House and referred to as "soluble coffee". After the war, it was marketed as "instant coffee" by Maxwell.

In 1943, Americans were told to "use it up, wear it out, make it do or do without." On February 7, shoes were rationed. You could only purchase three pairs a year. Most shoe retailers cut back on their advertising.

Because of the rationing of paper, newspapers and magazines could not accomodate all the advertising. By using light weight paper, magazines were able to carry many of the ads submitted to them. As for newspapers, they began to use "split-runs", whereby one advertiser occupied a certain space in half the edition and another occupied the same space in the other half. Remember, in those years most major dailies used to publish morning and evening editions.

At one point early in the war, Washington had considered advertising non-deductible as a business expense. Fortunately, many of the companies which depended upon advertising cooperated with the government by scheduling ads or incorporating in their ads "public service copy" urging people to invest money in war bonds, conserve rubber and fuel, recycle tin, etc.. By donating space or radio time towards the war effort, Washington allowed businesses to deduct most of their advertising as a legitimate business expense. It has been estimated that close to $1 billion in space and broadcast time was utilized for public service advertisement.

During the war, the American advertising industry founded the War Advertising Council, a nonprofit public-service organization employing the resources of modern advertising to strengthen the war effort. After the war, the organization continued as The Advertising Council to function in the public interest. It has conducted, for example, nationwide drives to increase the sale of United States Savings Bonds, prevent forest fires and traffic accidents, promote religion and encourage aid to higher education. Print and broadcast media contributed about $463 million worth of advertising time and space to such projects. Twenty six advertising agencies contributed their creative services to all the Council's campaigns.

No question about it, advertising played an important role during the war years. Ad agency talent contributed towards numerous patriotic causes, such as War Bond drives. Many leading advertisers devoted ad space towards boosting the morale of the country or to promote Defense Bonds and Stamps. For example, a Timken Bearing ad was headlined, "Help Strangle Hitler." Wrigley Chewing Gum transit and outdoor posters urged readers to invest money in bonds and stamps, while H. J. Heinz ran an ad asserting, "Blame Hitler, Hirohito and Benito."

Public relations also grew up during the war years. Hitler should be given credit as one of the few heads of government recognizing the importance of saturating the people with propaganda and special events, such as staging parades and mass calesthenics. Hitler recognized the importance of pageantry and dramatic effects. He would have had a more successful life as a public relations or marketing expert. There's no doubt about it. Hitler understood the frailties of humans and took full advantage. The use of the Nazi swastika became as popular as the Christian and the Red Cross logos. A review of their materials proves they had expert knowledge of typography, photographic color separation, and more. Volumes of propaganda literature were produced, including picture books, posters, and banners.

The propaganda/public relations geniuses of the Nazi regime proved people could be motivated and turned into "believers". Hitler, some will say, was a madman; others will say he was a genius; others still say he was an expert on human behavior. Whatever, he certainly was evil.

Public relations—or propaganda—in the U.S. largely emanated from Hollywood. The public was treated to constant barrages of public relations programs, especially propaganda movies aimed at keeping up the public morale. Today, many of those films are shown on television; in hindsight, they are interesting when viewed in a dispassionate way. These films were very effective, and proved to be a most valuable public relations tool.

Back to me and the war.

Chapter Seven

The evening of March 31, 1944, we boarded the Mauretania at a pier in New York. It was a British luxury liner converted into a troop ship. The Red Cross assigned a dozen or more women to give us paperbacks and playing cards as we filed up the gang plank to board the ship. It was a quiet scene since many of us were lost in our own personal thoughts. As I took the first step on the gang plank, I thought of my family and whether I would ever return home.

Once on board, we were directed by British merchant marines to take a stairway leading to the bowels of the ship. That would be our living quarters. We would sleep there, eat there, and, literally, be confined there for the entire trip. We slept in hammocks strung to pipes on the ceiling. The place was crowded and stuffy.

Once bunkered down, the speculation began: where the hell are we headed? North Africa? Iceland? England? A bit later, we were informed we would be crossing the Atlantic alone, without an escort. We were also told that the Mauretania's speed could out-distance enemy submarines. Great comfort!

And so our journey began. As we slowly made our way out into the Atlantic, the public address system was activated. We listened carefully to the instructions. "There'll be no smoking on deck. Do not toss anything overboard since it will alert the enemy of our presence." That really scared us. Suddenly, I had all these creepy thoughts that we were surrounded by enemy submarines!

The following morning, we were told we were heading for England, due to arrive at Liverpool on April 8. The news was good and we all cheered, as North Africa was not very appealing—you can well imagine. So, for nine days, we roamed the crowded below-decks area as best we could, played poker, read paperbacks, and talked about what life must be like in merry olde England.

Meanwhile, back in Boston, a bus strike was in progress, state Treasurer Francis X. Hurley announced he would be a candidate for governor, Spencer Shoes was advertising women's shoes for $3.65 a pair, and genuine leather handbags were selling for $1.99. At Boston's Colonial Theatre, Bela Lugosi was appearing on stage in "Arsenic and Old Lace". Lugosi would later achieve fame and notoriety as "Count Dracula".

On arriving in Liverpool, we were given some reading material, including a War Department booklet entitled, "If you should be captured, these are your rights." We were told to read it and study it thoroughly. Which we did. The last piece of advice in the 19-page booklet was, "Your own pride as a soldier will see you through." I read that over and over again, trying to figure out just what it meant.

I did not appreciate that a prisoner of war, privates and privates first class, must work in labor parties as ordered. Talk about discrimination!

The booklet included illustrations of German officers questioning a captured GI. . .they looked mean! We were instructed to forget all we ever knew about our army. I still have that booklet—I hid it in one of the storage boxes in my jeep. Often, I wondered who its illustrator and copywriter was. Former advertising people? Possibly, because it was well done.

Having arrived in Liverpool, I was sent to the European Civil Affairs Center and School in Shrivenham located in the heart of England. I soon learned that I'd be part of a small unit which would participate with the invasion of France to assist in civilian control. We were also being trained to act as a military government unit once in Germany. Our unit would consist of experts in the fields of municipal administration, industry and the arts. Where did I fit into this? I would be an assistant as well as a jeep driver.

For years, I have wondered how I wound up as a member of a crack unit which scored "top intelligence" ratings in the army classification test at induction. My army intelligence test was scored average. To be tossed in the middle of officers and some enlisted men who had college degrees will continuously puzzle me.

We were billeted in small cottages, six to a cottage. Our mess hall was located close to a half-mile away. To rouse us out of bed at 5 a.m., a GI would come through the area beating on a bass drum!

We discovered a lengthy article in *The Stars & Stripes* about our unique mission which, according to the story, had been kept secret. The article pretty much covered our daily activities that included classes, firing range practice with carbines, pistols and tommy guns. We were startled to read we had been assigned to a combat unit to accompany it on the invasion. The article was date-lined April 25. Thanks to the article, we had a better and clearer understanding of our mission and role in the upcoming invasion of the Continent.

General Eisenhower came to visit us and we duly sat on the ground, listening to him. All I remember from his talk was that the time was getting closer to our attacking German forces in Europe. "The time was getting closer?" I wasn't listening anymore! It all sort of felt unreal. During this whole period, from the time I was drafted, to being assigned to Camp Swift,

to crossing the Atlantic and arriving in England, the war itself
seemed to be happening on another planet. I hadn't witnessed a
bombing or heard a bullet whiz past me or seen a grenade
explode at my feet. But General Eisenhower's speech suddenly
brought the reality close to all of us, and it hit me real hard. To
tell the truth, I was scared. This fright was heightened as we
began hearing enemy planes overhead at night, dropping their
bombs. Many a night we jumped from our beds and rushed
outside to lie in a ditch on hearing enemy planes.

Some time later, we were transferred to Manchester where
we were billeted in civilian homes in Fallowfield, a suburb of
Manchester, my home being 63 Derby Road, owned by the
McCormicks, a husband, a wife, and son. While there, I fell
madly in love for the first time in my fading teens. She
was. . .but, that's another story, for another time—maybe!

Off to France.

Chapter Eight

In September of 1944, our unit was holed-up in Rochefort, France, the property of a large well-appointed chateau. As we waited orders for our next assignment, we killed time by having bullshit sessions around a small camp fire, or wrote letters or just smoothed out our sleeping quarters—oversized foxholes. Among the members of the unit, I was singled out as a yapper. True, I was continuously talking about my experiences in high school and as a musician. For a guy who was looking at 20 and the baby of the outfit, I was never at a loss for words!

Our outfit consisted of 26 individuals, half of whom were officers. I learned quite a bit from them about the goals of our mission, since many of them in civilian life were professionals—lawyers, judges, engineers, etc.—and they were very articulate. I learned geo-politics, as well as governmental organization. In short, they taught me how to keep a town or city alive and on the move.

Three days before our orders to move out, I took off with another member of the outfit whose name was Alvin. He was 25 and had been to college and knew some French. We left for Paris, which had recently been liberated, after having received permission by our commanding officer. We made it on our own to Paris by hitching rides on army trucks. The reason we got the pass was because we had a twig drawing contest and the two who picked the shortest twigs were the winners. So it was off to

Paris for a day and a night! When we got there, there was still sporadic shooting. Snipers prevailed in some spots, but Alvin and I didn't fear anything—Hell! We were in Paris!

There we were, two grubby looking GIs who hadn't had a bath in months, carrying carbines, and an extra pack of cigarettes to entice the French girls. I left it up to Alvin to call the shots, such as where to head for. Alvin said we'd go to Pigalle, and so we made our way toward the Eiffel Tower.

Suddenly, we were greeted by sniper fire and immediately hit ground. I could see the Eiffel Tower just ahead and I said, "Alvin, let's make a run for the Tower. Be safer there."

We got up and ran like hell, zig-zag fashion, until we reached our goal, and hid behind one of the steel legs of the Tower. We were panting heavily, but soon noticed the sniper fire had ceased. In about ten minutes, we were joined by three other GIs, whom Alvin asked for directions to Pigalle. One of them told us how to get there, and we took off, passing the Cathedral of Notre Dame, before finally reaching our destination.

The street was quiet in late afternoon, and we wondered where the girls were. Then from out of the Hotel D'Italia, three lovely young women rushed us, hugging and kissing us. I could hardly believe this was really happening. It was like a fantasy, make-believe. The rest? Well, that's my private history!

Back in Rochefort, we awaited further orders, as we spent most of the day bullshitting about many things, including the hope that Hitler would soon surrender to end the war.

During daylight hours, we were allowed to start fires to heat coffee. One morning, as we sat around on the ground by the small fire, one of the officers mentioned the name of Gertrude Stein, wondering if she was still in Paris or if she had been captured by the Germans. "Who is Gertrude Stein?" I asked.

"She's an American who wrote 'a rose, is a rose, is a rose'", the officer replied.

I thought it was a pretty stupid line and, being a wise guy, I said, "Yeah, a bullet is a bullet is a bullet. Does this make me a famous poet?"

It was good for a few laughs. (Coincidentally, I later learned that Gertrude Stein was first published in America by Four Seas, the forerunner of Branden Publishing Company, which also published the first work of William Faulkner. You see, I'm in pretty good company.)

Who would think in years to come I would have a love affair with Gertrude? I read much of what she wrote, and what others wrote about her. I even began to write a "one act" play bringing her back to life. In 1974, I visited her grave in Pierre Lachaise Cemetery in Paris and placed some flowers on her grave. Funny, the way things happen in life.

I was fortunate to have been part of a military unit made up of well educated men. Being the baby of the outfit and with only a high school education, I learned by listening (that's right, I didn't always talk) to the others talk about Dos Passos, James Joyce, George Bernard Shaw, and many other literary giants. But it wasn't all one-sided! Many a time the guys would ask me about big bands, and I educated them on the likes of Tommy Dorsey, Bob Crosby, Duke Ellington, Harry James and many others. I became the authoritative voice on music!

On November 15, our unit moved into Alsdorf, Germany, which was under enemy artillery and mortar fire. The front was 500 yards from where we settled for the night, taking refuge in the basement of what was left of an old building used as coal mine offices. Early the next morning, enemy mortar shells exploded nearby, one bursting outside the building, killing a captain and wounding a major and a corporal. We ran for cover in the basement.

Mid-morning the next day, an enemy mortar shell burst just outside our headquarters, killing another officer and wounding three GIs. Minutes before, I was standing in the doorway, lighting up a cigarette. With the butt dangling from my mouth, I assisted the wounded by moving them inside. Expecting more shelling, we headed down to a bunker into the building.

On November 21 at 2:45 a.m., enemy artillery began pounding again, shells exploding like firecrackers of a Fourth of July. I was knocked off my feet by one of the explosions, which severely wounded one of our officers. We all scrambled down to a mine shaft for cover. The next morning there was more shelling, forcing us to stay in the coal mine. This went on for another day until our artillery and aircraft pummeled the enemy positions.

A few days later, our infantry was prepared to cross a field to try and capture the town of Julich. I shook hands with some of the guys, wishing them luck. As the infantry moved across the field, enemy fire opened up on them, picking off some of the GIs. I kept shouting to them to "hit the ground!" but they couldn't hear because of the machine gun fire and shells exploding all around.

After a hard-fought battle, we captured Julich.

It was during this period I was told to drive back to Holland to deliver a pouch of reports to headquarters. It was a cold, sunny day as I drove down one of the few roads considered safe. On my way back, I thought it was all over for me, that my luck had run out. On hearing gunfire, I slowed down, sweeping my eyes along the terrain. There was a farmhouse not too far away, maybe 50 yards or so. Then I heard the gunfire again and saw the German near the door.

I jammed on the brakes and jumped over the side, down a ditch to take cover. Quickly, I crawled up, to take a peek. I was afraid of what I would see, envisioning hordes of Germans

coming at me, opening fire. "So this is how it's going to end!" I
thought. "Alone in a deserted area. Well, I won't give up
without a fight to the end."

I raised my Thompson sub-machine gun, poised to fire
away, my mouth dry with fear. Then I heard a Jeep rumbling
down the road, to my right—the greatest sight I ever witnessed! Inside were two GIs who had spotted my Jeep tilted to
the side of the road. They stopped and came to my aid as I
yelled, "Take cover! There's enemy in the farmhouse!"

They joined me in the ditch, where I explained I had seen a
German in the farmhouse. We decided to start opening fire at
the farmhouse to see results it would produce. It worked. In a
few minutes, the German soldier appeared in the yard, holding
his hands in the air.

"Ich bin allein. Ich bin allein," he continued to shout.

When I got up to him, I yelled, "You bastard, you tried to
kill me. I should shoot you apart."

The GIs told me I could take off, that they would take him
in. Before crawling back into my Jeep, I told them, "Look,
don't do him in. It could mean bad luck for all of us."

As I drove off, I looked back and felt better seeing the
German being hustled into the Jeep.

Daily, we came under enemy artillery fire. Once, I was
taking a cold water shave, using my steel helmet as a basin,
when a shell hit nearby. I quickly put my helmet on—water
and suds—and headed for cover in the basement of the building. We survived the shelling without any injuries or damage
to our vehicles. The enemy artillery and bombing became a
daily challenge to survive, though. And then, almost without
warning, around December 18, the shelling and bombing
eased up greatly, and we were optimistic about winning, now.

"Victory is a strange and wonderful thing. To each man it is something differnt, something personal. In many respects, it is like a heady drink. The effects are sudden and inspiring. But the after-effects are apt to be slow and depressing."

Archibald McLeish, *Meaning of Victory*

Chapter Nine

New Year's Day 1945: It was early morning, cold and the sun was just rising. It was quiet. No sounds of artillery or gunfire anywhere. As we were crossing a debris-littered street, a German plane came slowly out of the sky, swooping down over us. On receiving our fire, it began to bank. When it turned to make another run at us, we spotted smoke poring out of its fuselage. "We hit it! We hit it!" we yelled. The plane began gliding towards the ground when the pilot suddeny bailed out. He wasn't wearing a parachute, and even if he had had one, it wouldn't have helped him because he was too close to the ground. Within seconds, the plane hit the ground and burst into a dazzling ball of fire. We rushed over and found the lifeless body of the pilot. Kaput! We began wondering why he hadn't bothered to strafe us. We speculated he was either drunk or suffering from a New Year's hangover.

New Year's Day dinner was the usual fare—K or C rations. None of us wished one another a Happy New Year; it would have sounded hollow. Happy New Year? It was just another day in our lives.

Meanwhile, on New Year's Day, 1945, most Bostonians, who had a son, brother or relative fighting in Europe, were concerned about the German Army's counter-offensive, which would become known as "The Battle of the Bulge". The news from the front was encouraging. General Patton's Third Army had launched a full-scale offensive of the Belgian town of Bastogne.

Bostonians ushered in the New Year with enough uproar to awaken the Pilgrim Fathers, reported Stanley Eames of The *Boston Herald*.

We sensed the war in Europe was coming to an end when the U. S. 9th Army crossed the Rhine opposite Dusseldorf on March 6, 1945, linking up with the 1st Army and capturing close to 350,000 Germans. From that day on my outfit was continuously on the move, rushing into German cities and towns, trying to keep the civilian population under control.

On April 21, our unit was ordered to move fast to Wuppertal. Without sleep, we pushed our small convoy of jeeps and trucks for days and nights, our only rest coming on "latrine calls".

We entered Wuppertal, then under the control of the Arrowhead Infantry Division, and immediately began with our chore of putting the city of a half million people back on its feet. In less than four weeks, we succeeded in returning water service to approximately 90 percent of the residential city, getting the street railways and railroads back in action.

In Wuppertal, I also had the honor of "requisitioning" a large home on Funke Strasse for our headquarters. After many months of sleeping in cellars or on the ground, we finally had a decent roof over our heads, plus a large kitchen to warm up our K and C rations.

My most pleasurable experience was the recruitment of Frauleins to do the housekeeping and cooking for us. I selected three young, attractive ones, promising them food and cigarettes in return for their services.

Not only was I in charge of the Frauleins, but also of a stray puppy I found wandering over the debris of a shelled-out home. I named him Wuppy and kept him in my quarters, fattening him up on K-rations. Before leaving Wuppertal, I presented the frisky puppy to Lotte, one of our Frauleins.

Later, we got orders to proceed immediately to the birthplace of Nazism—Munich. Again, we underwent gruelling hours of driving over shelled-out or bombed out roads. It was a long journey from Wuppertal to Munich, and I came close to saying, "auf widerschen" to the world. Here's what happened.

Dogged tired from travel, I fell asleep at the wheel. When I awoke, I was pitched over a deep ravine, the Jeep literally balancing at the edge of the steep drop. I think if I had moved my body forward, both Jeep and I would have toppled over.

Just then, I heard voices shouting, "Don't move! Stay just as you are!"

I sat frozen in the spot, waiting for my buddies to hook up a winch from a two and a half ton truck to the back of the Jeep. Slowly, the winch pulled the Jeep back to safety. Whew! What was a close call! It was then decided we should all take a break: "Take ten!"

In Munich, I assisted Captain Borom to head up the restoration of utilities, transportation and communications. The following is recorded in our unit's history: "During the early days in Munich, the efficiency and humor of the section was greatly increased by the assignment of Corporal Barisano as second in command."

And so, a Captain and a Corporal worked together getting Munich moving again. Captain Borom proved to be a great educator, explaining to me with great patience our objectives. I am indebted to him for his confidence in me.

Our unit's history also included this item about us: "The
Captain and Corporal are awaiting orders for their former pro-
fessions, namely, fishing in Georgia and drumming in
Boston."

Munich was a holiday for us. For living quarters, we com-
mandeered a large mansion owned by a German general. It also
included a swimming pool and servants' quarters, which our
officers occupied. Again, I had the delightful assignment of
"hiring" two young Frauleins to do our laundry and other
housekeeping chores.

In 1945, as the war was coming to an end, eight new public
relations agencies were launched in Boston, bringing the total
number to 19. Opening for business in 1945 were: Newsome
and Company, with offices at 9 Newbury Street. One of the
hottest agencies during that time was Harry Paul Associates,
located at 80 Boylston Street—Harry's home for over 40 years.

Some of the popular restaurants, and so-called hot spots
which advertising and p.r. executives frequented were: Bob
Berger's, at 256 Tremont Street, featuring frog legs, shad roe,
soft shell crabs and the ever-popular one-pound steaks, and the
Hotel Essex, opposite South Station, where for $1 you could
enjoy a full course dinner. What's more, there was dancing at
the Essex, plus floor shows. Other favorite spots were Cafe De
Paris, Freda's, Boraschi's and The Viking on Stuart Street.

The growth of ad agencies between 1941 and 1945 was
minimal, with only 83 agencies listed in the Boston Yellow
Pages. Out of that total, only 35 were considered full-service
firms.

When the war in Europe came to an end, American soldiers
occupying Germany were instructed not to fraternize with
Germans, specifically with the Frauleins. For many of us, our
minds said do not fraternize, but our young hearts urged us to

pursue the Frauleins with abandon. And so, fraternization became a big headache for Army brass. In order to combat or discourage the practice of fraternization, the army embarked on a public relations program of its own. It began distributing literature describing in graphic detail some of the atrocities committed by the enemy. The literature further exclaimed: "Don't visit in German homes, drink with Germans, shake hands with them, play games with them, give or accept gifts or attend social functions."

Did the p.r. gimmick work? Like hell it did! Fraternization continued at an increasing pace. There is one case that, I feel, needs to be told. A corporal, who was a Jew, said he fraternized with the Frauleins with the hope of impregnating them. "I'm going to make it possible for one of them to give birth to a kid with Jewish blood," he said.

And it happened! I was the first to know it since the corporal had been shipped home and the Fraulein he'd been dating came to see me, asking for his state-side address. I had taken a crash course in German so I asked her why. "Ich haben ein kinder," she replied.

So, he had succeeded in what he'd set out to do. I told her it was *verboten* to disclose the address of American soldiers. After this I dropped the bomb! "He's married to a wonderful Jewish woman."

She then asked if he was Jewish. "Yes, he is Jewish," I answered. She broke into tears and left.

Years later, when working in New York, I tracked him down. We got together at a small restaurant in the Wall Street district, and reminisced about our war-time experiences. As we were leaving, I said: "By the way, did you know that after you left that Fraulein you'd been dating came to ask me for your home address. She wanted to tell you she was pregnant."

He shook his head. "I wonder if she had a boy or girl?" Then added: "To think there's a kid in Germany with some Jewish blood. I did it! I did it!" he exclaimed jubilantly.

On August 10, Japan sued for peace, bringing an end to World War II. So began the lengthy process of discharging millions of Americans from military service, our thoughts immediately set on seeing our families again. It had been close to three years since I'd seen mine. Besides, I neither had a job nor any idea what I'd be doing once home. But none of that really bothered me.

I made *The Stars and Stripes* on September 27, 1945. What a thrill! The paper carried a story about how our unit held a "grand anniversary party" in Munich, which I had organized. I requisitioned the booze, musicians and a large cake. It was quite an evening. I also took over the drums, making it my first experience playing with German musicians.

One of the guys took a photo of me reading old editions of *Down Beat* magazine. We sent the photo to the magazine, and was published in its November 1, 1945 issue. Finally, I had made it in *Down Beat*!

Corporal Seymour Shepcaro, my roommate, sent the photo to the magazine, with a blurb about my being known as "Ray Barron, his drums and orchestra", also noting that I had participated in four battles. Well, let me say this: I have purposely elected not to go into detail about my war experiences. They are mostly the same—stories of death and survival. Like the other soldiers in the war, we learned how fragile we all are. When death is around, we mourn to ourselves in silence. One time, however, I mourned loudly.

It happened after the war, while visiting the American cemetery in Soisson, France, to say goodbye to a friend. When I found the white wooden cross with his dogtag nailed on it, I suddenly began shouting. "I made it! You stupid bastard! I made it!" I cried, out of control.

I was the only living American in the cemetery on that damp, drizzly morning, mad as hell. Mad because so many young Americans were cheated out of living a full cycle. Needing to release my pent-up emotions, I resorted to yelling and to cursing them all for dying.

I will never forget my visit to the lonely American cemetery. I tried to control my emotions, but the sight of the hundreds of white crosses and Stars of David was too much to bear. As I walked away on that gray morning, I paused, turned around and began to shout, "See you later guys!" My eyes filled with tears, I cried unashamedly.

One night, we received word that some of us would be heading home. That was cause for celebration, and we all got smashed on cognac. Gulping down the drinks, we reminisced about some of our experiences together. Soon, we began to admit to each other the many moments we felt like breaking down and having a good cry. Self pity? Possibly. I remember breaking down one night as I was standing guard while the wind-swept snow began to cover me. Wet and freezing, all I could think of was being back home in my bed under blankets with a soft pillow to rest on. How much more of this can I take? I wondered. I wish I was dead. But I got it all out of my system as I stood guard that night. Whenever the Germans shot up a flare, I would think of the fireworks display at the Italian festivals in East Boston. And the tears would flow again.

It wasn't until December 12, 1945 that we boarded the Mariposa in Marseilles, France for the trip home. We slipped out of the pier on a bright sunny morning for what would turn out to be a stormy crossing. Our destination was Hampton Roads, Virginia. Out in the middle of the Atlantic, we encountered mountainous waves which created mass sea sickness aboard ship. The Mariposa was bobbing in the ocean like a cork and it was rumored that one of its plates had been sprung and was taking water. Fortunately, I held up and was able to assist some of the seasick soldiers.

At the height of the storm, I coaxed another GI to join me on deck to have a picture taken. Storm or no storm, I figured this was a momentous occasion. After all, how many times do you get too fight in a war and board a ship for home?

We got on deck as the ship continued to lunge upwards and then smashing down into a gaping valley, only to be swept up by the huge waves. Wearing life jackets, we held on to the sides of the ship for dear life. I began to think this is a hell of a thing: I had survived the war, to drown at sea!

Anyway, we endured and took turns taking the other's picture, which I prized among the many others. It was worth the effort—and the risk!

At Hampton Roads, tugboats welcomed us back to America, by blasting their horns. As we tied up to the pier, hundreds of people shouted joyously, "Welcome back!" It was truly a moving site. As I took my first step on American soil in what seemed like an eternity, I thought of the guys left behind. You'll never be forgotten, I assured them.

We arrived at Fort Patrick Henry by train. It was dark. As we tramped over the ground, lights suddenly went on and a military band struck up a spirited marching song. It was a surprise welcome back home tribute. We marched up to a camp auditorium where a colonel, on stage, gave us the good news: we would all be speedily processed for discharge. But, first, he added, we would be treated to steak and ice cream in the mess hall. We cheered the colonel. This was to be our first steak and ice cream in years. Another piece of good news was that we would be allowed to make a three-minute long distance phone call home. More cheering.

Our only disappointment came on learning we wouldn't be discharged in time to be home for Christmas. But it really didn't bother me because I had missed three Christmases while in the Army.

On December 30, 1945, I was discharged from the U.S. Army at Fort Devens, Massachusetts. At 6 o'clock in the evening, along with two other "ex GIs", I took a cab from Devens to Boston. I would be heading to Orient Heights, East Boston, the other two for North Station to take trains to New Hampshire and Maine.

As the cab made its way over snow covered streets heading for 1132 Saratoga Street, I thought of how it would be like being back in my own bedroom, back to privacy, seeing my family again. . .how I would adjust to civilian life. . .and what I would be doing for a living.

Although the thought had never entered my mind, I had changed over the course of the years in the army. I had grown up—immediately.

Back to my musical career.

Chapter Ten

After the war, I resumed my career in music at night while attending Burdett College daytime. That's when I discovered what advertising was all about, as one of the required courses was advertising. Our instructor was an account executive at Harry Frost Advertising, one of Boston's largest agencies. I enjoyed his lectures immensely, as well as the text book on advertising. Little did I know that the course would have a profound impact on me in the 50s, an serve as a bright beacon for my future career in advertising.

But music was what really occupied my heart in the years after the war. I did everything from leading a band, to running a nightclub to promoting visiting celebrities, including Lionel Hampton. I remember the time I appeared on Norm Nathan's show at WMEX Radio with Lionel, who tried to explain what "Bebop" was all about. He went on for a while until I began to butt in, crediting Stravinsky as the man who inspired Bebop, and drawing looks of amazement from both Lionel and Norm.

My love for Bebop, or Progressive Jazz, was not in vain. I used to stage Bebop Jazz Concerts, starring local bop musicians, at the Hi-Hat Club. When I worked and lived in New York, I managed Bebop combos and met with some success in obtaining recording contracts and bookings. But Bebop never caught on, and there are numerous reasons why. Some say bop musicians were always on drugs, a bunch of freaked out musi-

cians. True, drugs—especially pot—were widely used by musicians during the 40s and 50s.

Perhaps the best explanation why it failed is in Ira Gittler's
book, *Swing to Bop* published by Oxford University Press,
1985. The volume ends with an incident concerning me—how
in 1951, I tried to book Red Rodney's Bebop band, only to
have the nightclub owner hang up on me. Nightclub owners
apparently felt Bebop bands were too risky, that there wasn't a
wide audience for tha kind of music.

As a musician, music columnist and manager of talent, I had
the opportunity to meet many famous jazz musicians. The list
is endless: Count Basie, Buddy Rich, Gene Krupa, Prez Prado,
Zoot Sims, Stan Getz, Buddy De Franco, Sammy Davis Jr.,
Miles Davis, Gerry Mulligan, Terry Gibbs, Stan Kenton, Guy
Lombardo, Tony Pastor, Claude Thornhill, Benny Goodman,
Duke Ellington, Erroll Garner, and many others with whom I
broke bread, smoked pot with, or helped to get them gigs or
publicity.

One short lived experience happened on being hired as a
manager of Louie's Lounge, located at the corner of Northamp-
ton and Washington Streets in Boston's South End. It was to be
my first and last experience as a nightclub manager.

The Lounge was a lively evening spot in 1948, featuring
"colored acts", and I was its only visible "offay". The owner,
Louie Fortinalis, was never around and trusted me to keep
things under control. My assistant was a tough-looking black
named Lucky, who also served as a bouncer.

My first week as the big shot manager of Louie's, I decided to
have Art Tacker, a disc jockey at WTAO in Cambridge, do a
remote from the Lounge from 4 to 5 p.m. This was done to
stimulate early business and to attract whites to the place. I
instructed Art never to mention on air that I was the manager,

as I feared my mother and stepfather would have a fit if they heard about my managing a colored nightclub.

The Art Tacker remote proved to be a flop. The only people around at that hour were heavy drinkers who could care less about some white guy spinning records and talking into a microphone. After two weeks, I canceled the remote.

As club manager, I used to patrol the tables to make sure the waitresses were hustling drinks. I was also clocking the small house band and the acts to make sure they didn't goof off. One act, a tap dancer who was to be on stage for the first show, didn't appear. Instead, he was in the small dressing room making love to one of the waitresses. Lucky discovered the pair through a peep hole and informed me about the situation. I banged on the door and told them both to get out or we would smash the door down. It was quite a scene! I didn't fire the waitress because she was known for being popular with the customers, and allowed the dancer to go on stage, do his thing, and forget the whole matter.

But as time went on, I became increasingly frustrated with the daily nuisance of running a nightclub. There were many fights and, more frequently, drunks had to be tossed out. We never called the police because that would only give the place a bad name. So, out they went, head first into the side alley.

Then one night, I caught this guy lifting a billfold from a patron. Following him to the men's room, and seeing him quickly rifling through the stolen billfold, I ordered him to hand it over. Big mistake! Suddenly, I was staring at a glinting knife. In a mad dash, I rushed out of the bathroom and got hold of Lucky, who went after the thief. Struggling to the floor, Lucky was able to wrest the knife from the thief. With the patrons on their feet applauding, Lucky tossed the thief into the alley.

Shaken by the incident, the next day I told the owner I was through at Louie's.

While staging concerts at the Hi-Hat Club, I met Herb Frank, of Herbert Frank Advertising. He was handling the advertising for the popular jazz club. Herb's advertising agency was also known for handling restaurants, nightclubs, hotels and resorts. Julie Rosenberg, the owner of Hi-Hat used to show me Herb's ads and asked what I thought of them. Rarely did I have to recommend changes. Some of the ads included my name in bold type face which, of course, pleased me.

I also got to know Harry Paul, of Harry Paul Associates, who was handling the publicity for the Hi-hat. I first met Harry when he was doing publicity for the Down Beat Club on Tremont Street, where I staged weekly jazz concerts. Harry used to get after me to mention in my *Down Beat* columns some of the other clubs he was handling.

Another individual at the Club was the illustrious graphic designer George Campbell, who acted as a *maitre d'* of the club. He would some day be part of my career in advertising, as we both, ultimately, worked together at Dowd Advertising.

At the Hi-Hat, I was first introduced to Malcolm X, the charismatic black separatist, then living in Boston. He used to frequent the Hi-Hat, usually alone. We always talked about jazz, never politics. My impression of him was that he was a serious type of guy who rarely showed emotions. We got along just fine.

As time went on, I began to lose enthusiasm for the life of a musician. One incident clearly understates my growing need to do something else. In the summer of 1950 Joe Holicker, a graduate of Boston University College of Music and an accomplished musician, asked if I would like to be a drummer of a house band in a nightclub on Cape Cod. Joe explained the money would be good and the gig would include accomodations in a cottage located near the beach.

"Ray, you'll enjoy the summer at the Cape and we'll have a ball. Johnny Dimenico will be on trumpet and there'll be a great pianist, Lenny Davis," Joe said.

We checked into the cottage a week before the season opened at Casa Madrid, a large Spanish style building located in West Yarmouth. The Casa, we were told, catered to the elite, the very rich. As the house band, we would be playing seven nights a week, two floor shows a night, plus music for dancing. Our evening began at seven and ended at one a.m., except Saturdays when we quit at 12 midnight in observation of the "Sabbath law".

Holicker was right about the summer being a ball. We were young, single with the exception of Lenny Davis, and there were parties galore. We had no problem meeting well-bred vacationing young women, either. For some reason, they always seem attracted to musicians. Anyway, we spent lazy days on the beach, and after work, pursued our adventures with women bent on summer romances.

Then came Labor Day, and the end of our Casa Madrid gig. On packing my drums, I mentioned to Holicker that this might be my last gig as a drummer. Stunned, he asked, "But why? What are you talking about?"

"I've about had it. I really don't enjoy sweating night after night as a drummer", I explained.

It was true: I was neither a Buddy Rich nor a Gene Krupa—that was the problem, and I had a keen idea of my limitations. I wasn't bad, but. . . And the work itself—the exhaustion it produced was wearing me down.

Back home, I stored my drums away in the basement and decided to get involved in the business end of music. There was an opportunity to work in a hotel in Pensacola, Florida, with my own group, but I wired back to the booking agent refusing the winter long engagement. I have often wondered what would have followed if I had continued to work as a musician.

Later, I went to New York where I met my future wife, Marilyn, and ultimately—and severely—cut back on my musical activities. Soon after, we came to Boston, where I worked my way into the advertising business, discovering I liked the creative part of advertising, writing copy that was eye-catching and appealing. I now own my own agency, live in Nahant with my lovely wife and two daughters. I have a lot to be grateful for. I've been blessed, for the 50s and the following decades bestowed upon me many wonderful happenings.

But it was the 40s that laid the groundwork for my later success. The 40s gave me character, direction; taught me a lot about life and the people who populate this universe of ours.

Clearly, the 40s made me wise and, hopefully, a person with a heart.

And now a word about some of the characters in Advertising.

Chapter Eleven

This book would not be complete without mentioning some of the memorable people engaged in advertising in Boston during the 40s. One of them, Arnold Rosoff, easily recalled his life and times as a young man breaking into the advertising business.

In 1939, and fresh out of Harvard, Rosoff was hired by David Malkiel, president of David Malkiel Advertising, located at 260 Tremont Street. Impressed by the young Rosoff, Malkiel assigned him to assist in the servicing of some of the agency's major accounts, such as Serta Mattress, Massachusetts Envelope Company and Boston Showcase. Rosoff was also deeply involved with creating ads for the accounts.

In early 1941, begging to be recognized in the advertising community as an astute and creative ad executive, he distinguished himself as a set designer for a new musical revue, "Baa Baa Back Bay" at the Charles Playhouse.

Like many others, he was drafted into the military, serving first with the Army's 26th Infantry Division, and later as an Air Force pilot. When the war ended, he returned to the Malkiel agency. Late in 1946, Rosoff launched his own agency, and the rest is history. I asked him why he went into the ad business. "It appealed to me at an early age", he said. "I was 12 years old and entered a drawing contest sponsored by the *Boston Herald*. I won the contest and got hooked on advertising."

One of the most colorful executives in the Boston advertising industry for over 65 years is Larry Shea. Born in 1896, he has spent his life working in the business. What's more, the energetic grand senior citizen of Boston's advertising community has survived three wars: The Mexican Border War, World War I and World War II. In speaking to Larry, I learned he was a classmate at Harvard Business School (after World War I) of Richard Humphrey, Sr., who also went on to distinguish himself as one of Boston's most prominent advertising executives.

On May 4, 1986, Larry celebrated his eighty-eighth birthday. While attending Harvard, Larry was told to try to get into the advertising business by one of his classmates. But it was his brother, a classmate of George Wiswell, who arranged for Larry to meet Wiswell, who had just launched his agency, Chambers & Wiswell.

According to Larry, he joined the agency on a commission basis. "I had to bring in business and was given a percentage of the net profit. I had what you call beginner's luck! I landed Cain's, the mayonnaise people, and New England Aviation a small 'airplane'." But Larry's luck didn't hold up too long, and Chambers & Wiswell gave him notice.

Larry Shea's next job was with the C. Brewster Smith advertising agency located at 25 School Street, Boston. Now a seasoned hustler, Shea picked up two new profitable pieces of business: The Greyhound Dog Track in Revere (now known as Wonderland Dog Track), and Cheyene's Vitamins of Boston. The young Larry Shea was enjoying the advertising business. As he put it, "I was bringing home enough money to support my wife and growing family."

On December 7, 1941, Larry and his friends were spending a Sunday afternoon playing touch football in Quincy when someone came running out to the field shouting, "The Japs have bombed Pearl Harbor!" It was a matter of time before the veteran of two previous wars would be called to serve his country once again. In early 1942, the call came, and Shea, a Lieutenant in World War I, was commissioned Captain in the U.S. Marine Air Corps.

After a short period of training, he joined the 2nd Marine Air Wing and saw action in the bloody battle of Okinawa in the South Pacific.

When the war ended, Shea decided to launch an advertising agency—Lawrence Associates with a small office at 84 State Street, Boston, a prestigious address, according to Larry. The year was 1946, and business was getting back to normal after five years of rationing of many products. One of the first accounts Larry pitched was the Greyhound Dog Track, the same account he had brought into the C. Brewster Smith agency, which continued to grow and expand during the forties and early fifties. The Lawrence agency became known as a good political advertising agency. Larry Shea handled John F. Kennedy's Congressional advertising campaign as well as that of Leverett Saltonstall's gubernatorial campaign.

Harold Segal, president of WNEB Radio in Worcester, one of New England's most respected broadcast executives, like most of us, found his life going in many directions during the forties. But in 1948, he discovered the direction to take. Let him speak for himself:

"In 1940 I was in my fourth year at BU Evening College of Commerce. In those days, one had to go six years at night for a degree. I was one of four sons, my father was a machinist and we had no extra money for education. It cost me $90 a semester. I worked during the day as a credit manager for a chain of stores called Cummings. I got $15 a week as a credit manager, Monday through Friday and Saturday until noon. Then Saturday afternoon I was sent to their store in Quincy where I worked until six o'clock Saturday night, for the same $15.

"On December 7, 1941, Pearl Harbor was attacked. I went down to enlist and I finished the first semester of my fifth year at Boston University Evening College on January 27th and went to Fort Devens on January 28, 1942. I was in North Africa, Sicily and Italy, overseas for a total of two and a half years and returned home in 1945. In February 1946, I returned to BU to complete the second semester of my fifth year. I graduated in June 1947, having completed the six year of academic requirements, though it took me ten years in total time.

"In 1946, while at BU, I took an elective course called 'Speech Training'. In those days I stammered and was not too clear in my speech. I was also recommended to a course called 'Radio Speech and Dramatics' where I talked into a microphone to learn proper breathing and pacing to slow my speech down.

"Our instructor, who worked at WEEI took us all to WEEI to watch a radio station in progress. The announcer on duty was Sherm Feller. Sherm was conducting a talk show, the first talk show in the city of Boston at that time. Sherm and I went to grammar school together in Roxbury and then to high school.

"Graduating from Boston University, I worked at Filene's Department Store in the credit department. At school I had met a young man who worked for a rug cleaning establishment who told me of the great opportunities of cleaning wall to wall carpeting which was becoming prevalent after World War II.

"I quit Filene's, we bought a truck, a vacuum and a scrubber and went out looking for work. It was a disaster! In December 1948 I was broke, having used up my savings from allotments I had coming to me from overseas and some other financial help I was able to obtain.

"Now I had to make a determination as to which direction I wanted to go and I was 31 years of age. Remembering the radio station visit, I felt that perhaps radio advertising might be the answer.

"Before Christmas 1948, I took a Greyhound bus to New York and I visited the four radio networks. At each network I was asked what I wanted to apply for, sales programming or engineering. I knew nothing about any of it and felt unqualified to be an announcer, knew nothing about engineering and never sold before. My last call was at ABC network. The personnel director, a Mr. VanDam advised me to go into sales and advised me to start at a small station.

"I returned home and went to WEEI. I met with Roy Marks, general sales manager, and Harold Fellows, general manager. Roy told me to go to a smaller station and recommended Brockton, Quincy or Cambridge. I did not have a car and felt I could commute better by streetcar or bus to Cambridge. I went to WTAO in Cambridge. The general manager was Paul Perreault. He wouldn't hire me without experience. He told me to go to a small station. His station was a 250 watt daytimer. I asked if there were smaller stations than his and he said no. I kept coming back and he kept refusing me. Finally, he told me he would hire me but would not pay me a salary or commission and he would see how I did. He gave me a rate card and assigned me to North Cambridge, Arlington and Belmont. Not having a car, I would use a bus to call on grocery stores, tailor shops, furniture stores, automobile dealers, brothels, garages, anything that would give me a sale. From January 9th until the first week in March I could not sell anything to anybody! In those days, two advertising periods were used. The spring and Easter as one period followed by the fall, Christmas and Thanksgiving season. In between, radio advertising, or advertising in general was curtailed. As a matter of fact, in those days they had a summer rate card for radio that reduced the rates in order to encourage people to advertise during the summer

"Ignorance being bliss, I went out every day and got my brains knocked out. I wanted to give up several times, but my wife insisted I could make it. Finally, in the first or second week in March 1949 I brought in 14 orders which was a record at the station at the time. I was then given $50 a week.

"In 1949 the advertising director of I. J. Fox Furriers in Boston called to tell me that there was going to be an opening at WCOP. One of the salesmen, Irving Hackmeyer was leaving to accept a job at WHDH. I was told to go over and meet with Harry Wheeler, Sales Manager of WCOP. I met with Harry and he said that they started salesmen off at $75 a week, but in my case he would offer me $50 a week as I did not have very much experience. I started at WCOP for Harry at $50 a week and a month or two later I got $75 a week. I stayed with WCOP until August of 1950 when Arthur Haley approached me to tell me he was putting WROL on the air and he asked me to come over as a salesperson. I accepted the job and it turned out to be one of the best decisions of my life."

Hirshon-Garfield Advertising, with offices in Boston's Park Square Building, was where Myron and Jason Silton broke into the advertising agency business. Myron was an account executive and Jason the agency's copy chief. Jason was with the agency for close to three years when Uncle Sam called him up. According to Jason, the agency handled footwear, fashion and food accounts. The agency was considered one of Boston's leading agencies employing 20 people.

Hirshon-Garfield was a New York agency and besides a branch in Boston, it also had an office in London. When the branch manager of the London office came to Boston, Jason and some other members treated him to lunch at the University Club. On being handed a menu, he looked it over, paused, then broke down and wept. In England, food was severely rationed with eggs, cheese, beef and fruits unheard of. Needless to say, our "British cousin", as they were called during the war years, enjoyed a hearty luncheon.

One of the most colorful characters active in the advertising agency business was Ernest Goulston of the Goulston Company located at 35 Court Street, Boston. Goulston was active in Boston politics and was known as a "King Maker". The short, well dressed Goulston was also referred to as "the Mayor of Beacon Hill". Volumes can be written about him, as a sharp advertising and public relations executive, as a womanizer, and as a millionaire who wound-up sharing office space with Harry Paul trying to eek out a living.

Though Jewish, he never practiced the faith. Some say he was a WASP; some call him a rogue. I did have the privilege to meet Ernest J. Goulston 28 years ago at his archaic looking offices and was deeply impressed by some of the work the agency had created for local and national accounts such as Boston Edison and Hayes Bickford. In short, he's the one who invented the future of advertising. On a personal note, Goulston advised me to always dress properly. "Remember, you're in the service business, dealing with principals of companies; so, try to reflect success and prosperity by dressing well."

One of the first Italian-Americans to own an advertising agency in Boston was Tony Cucchiara. In 1932, Tony had intended to pursue a career in law, but decided after one year to switch to the Massachusetts Institute of Advertising, a school offering two year courses in all phases of advertising. According to Tony, the faculty included working professionals such as Ed Parent and Dan Fox.

On graduating, Tony was hired by the *American Wool and Cotton Reporter*, a trade publication published in Boston. "My role at the magazine was to create ads for advertisers who did not have an advertising agency." After a year or so with the publication, Tony switched to *The New England Electric News* creating ads and writing feature stories. In 1937, the aspiring young advertising copywriter joined the Edmund S. Whitten advertising agency, one of Boston's top billing agencies as an account executive who, like all account executives during that era, doubled as copywriter and media planner.

One of Whitten's top billing was Carmote Paints. Tony reminded me that what was considered top billing accounts were companies with advertising budgets of $25 to $30 thousand.

In 1940, Tony, who was married, decided to launch an advertising agency, intending to name it *Anthony Cucchiara Advertising* but decided against it—it sounded too ethnic, and settled on Copley Advertising, opening for business at Boston's Park Square Building. He immediately went after schools and colleges which, according to Tony, were the easiest accounts to pitch.

When World War II broke out, Tony was deferred from military service because he was the father of two children. With young men being called up, many of the schools and colleges experienced a decline in enrollments. Tony was fortunate to have diversified his agency which had 40 schools and colleges as clients. Accounts that helped keep the agency alive and well were Kelley Shoe Polish, Seymour Ice Cream and three industrial accounts. One of the campaigns Tony created for Kelley—one of the largest makers of white shoe polish—was a tie-in with *Snow White and The Seven Dwarfs*, creating a half hour radio show on WEEI known as "The Snow White Parade".

One new account Copley Advertising acquired was Federal Distillers, creating a series of space ads promoting Federal's liquors which the client thought were great and immediately allocated $100,00 for space advertising. One problem, however, the rationing of paper forced publications to cut back their pages and to ration space to advertisers. Copley Advertising never did get all of the $100,000 earmarked for the campaign.

I asked Tony what advertising copywriters and art directors were paid weekly during those years. A salary of a copywriter was $30 and an art director $35. This was considered to be "high wages" during the thirties and the war years. One individual who commanded $30 a week was the late L. E. Sissman, who broke into business as a copywriter at Copley Advertising. It was through Ed Sissman I first met Tony Cucchiara when we were both working as copywriters at the John C. Dowd agency. Ed suggested I meet Tony, his former boss, to pick-up some possible freelance work. Yes, many of us "moonlighted".

Tony Cucchiara has had an interesting career in advertising. His reputation as one of Boston's leading advertising executives prompted Northeastern University to ask him to teach a course on the principles of advertising. Tony survived through the Depression and war years and says he has no regrets about choosing a career in advertising instead of law.

Harold Cabot & Company of Boston was perhaps the first advertising agency in America to have on staff a "radio time buyer"—Marion Goldie, who also doubled as a space buyer.

During the war years, Harold Cabot & Company maintained a branch office in Portland, Maine, headed by Frank Black. Some of Cabot's clients included: Boston University, Boston & Main Railroad, Chelsea Clock, Delano Potter & Company—tea and coffe packers, H.P. Hood, Arthur Murray Dance Studios, Stone & Webster and Newton Savings Bank.

The agency account executives: Harold Cabot, Don Douglas, John Kennedy, Bill Ganick, Ed Chase, Russell Hunt and Harvey Ford.

Oscar Bresnick, one of the pioneers of Boston's advertising industry, who retired in 1971 and went into the agency business in 1932, recalls the war years as those when advertising agencies began to grow. According to him, his agency, Bresnick & Solomont handled mostly retailers and manufacturers of shoes. The shortage of leather forced manufacturers of shoes to use synthetics for heels and soles. Some of Oscar's accounts included Wilbur Shoes, John Irving Shoes, Wilson Shoes and

Crosby Shoes. The agency had a staff of seven with Chet Solomont, Oscar's partner, serving as art director.

Chapter Twelve

Radio played an important role during the war years, and I'd like to devote this chapter to that medium and to some of its personalities.

In 1941, Boston had two active radio production houses: Fidelity Recording Studios and Kasper-Gordon Studios. Both houses created musical jingles and spots for many of leading retail stores, such as Filene's, Jordan, R. H. White's, Gilchrist's, Raymond's and Chandler's.

Boston radio stations programmed a wide variety of shows, many of which were remotes sponsored by restaurants and nightclubs. Quiz shows were also popular. The music stations played mostly big band stuff—recordings by Glenn Miller, Tommy Dorsey, Bob Crosby, Benny Goodman, Duke Ellington and many other swing bands.

Boston had two trade schools specializing in radio broadcast: Massachusetts Radio School and Massachusetts Television Institute. Both ran small space ads in Boston newspapers. The Television Institute promoted "Good jobs in radio"; Radio School headlined: "Learn Radio", which also included a line of copy, "Learn a trade for peace or war."

One local organization which still has records of their members is the American Federation of Television and Radio Artists, founded in Boston in 1938 as The American Federal Artists. In 1941, AFTRA had 57 members and four contracts with radio stations. Those helping to gain recognition for

AFTRA were: Fred B. Cole, Arch MacDonald, Ken Overden, Nelson Churchill, Grace Keddy, Ellie Dierdoff and Hal Newell, among others.

The first radio station to recognize AFTRA was WBZ, followed by WEEI, WNAC, and WHDH. In 1942, AFTRA banged out additional contracts with WCOP, WORL and WHDH. My mother's favorite radio personality was Fred B. Cole of WHDH. More than once, she told me Cole sounded like a nice guy—a handsome man. I suspect she had a crush on him

Speaking of Fred, in 1935 he walked in cold to WNAC, asking for a job as an announcer. He was just a young, brazen kid fresh out of Leland Powers School of Broadcasting and Acting in Boston. As luck would have it, the station was looking for an announcer. He was given an audition and hired on the spot! Working at the station was Bill McGrath, who would some day play an important role in Fred's illustrious career in radio.

After a year at WNAC, Fred was urged by two sales executives to leave and join them in a new radio station located by a cow pasture in Wellesley. According to Fred, when he reported for work, he was chased by a bull across the field! He then told the station owners he would not report to work unless they did something about that bull. As Fred described the station—it was an amateur radio station that used no call letters, but a frequency number which eventually became known as WROL, with studios in the Mayflower Hotel, located at Kenmore Square.

While at WROL, Fred heard of an opening for more money in Waterbury, Connecticut. Off he went to Waterbury, which eventually led to a job in Los Angeles, where he covered big band radio remotes from ballrooms.

Hardly a year out on the Coast, Fred was offered a job at WBZ. He was ecstatic to come back to Boston. It was Gordon Swain, program director of WBZ, who lured Fred back.

On Pearl Harbor Day, Fred was at home when the announcement came over the radio that the Japanese had bombed Pearl Harbor. He immediately left for the station, located at the Bradford Hotel on Tremont Street. Fred described that afternoon as sheer bedlam, with the majority of the staff monitoring news wires, and speculating about what would happen next.

With many young men being drafted or volunteering for military service, Fred was urged by an Army officer to join the Army's Intelligence Corps. Because of an injury to one of his eyes, Fred failed to pass the physical and instead took a job with the Office of War Information in New York, broadcasting reports on NBC's Blue Network. He says that much of what he reported was propaganda stuff.

In 1946, Bill McGrath, who had moved from WNAC to WHDH, offered Fred a job. Married at the time, Fred was hesitant to return to Boston because he and his wife enjoyed working and living in New York. But again, he thought it would be nice to be back home. It turned out to be a good decision when he did come back.

Bill Hahn, vice president of special projects for WRKO/WROR-FM has been employed by RKO General close to 44 years. A native of Rockford, Illinois, he attended Harvard, and says he'll never forget how during the outbreak of the war he came close to being tossed into prison for mentioning on his show on WROK in Rockford how beautiful the weather was—"clear skies and sunny". It was forbidden to talk about weather conditions since enemy planes could use the information to their advantage.

In 1942, as the war heated up, Bill found employment as a staff announcer at WCOP in Boston and also as a host of live radio programs. In 1943, he moved over to WHDH but left after 11 months to join WNAC and the Yankee Network. One of the shows Bill hosted was "The Answer Man" which was on the air across-the-board at 6:30 p.m. At 8:15 a. m., New Englanders tuned into "Breakfast with Bill" on the Yankee Network.

Bill Hahn has had an illustrious career in radio and television. As they say, he's done it all!

America's first late night radio talk show was launched in 1941, a week after Pearl Harbor, by WEEI with Sherm Feller as the host. The Sherm Feller Show was on the air each evening from 11:30 to 6 a. m. Sherm's show included guests, music and lots of talk about show business. Another reason why WEEI decided to broadcast throughout the evening was to provide "alerts". Immediately following the bombing of Pearl Harbor and the declaration of war, there was the fear of German sending planes to bomb our cities. Another fear was acts of sabotage. In 1943, Sherm was drafted into the Army Special Forces to help produce shows for the Army. Some of the people Sherm used for his entertaining shows included boxer Jack Dempsey, cowboy crooner Gene Autry, and comic Frank Fontaine.

In 1946, Sherm Feller returned to WEEI to once again host a talk show. It was at that time I first met him and his new bride Judy Valentine. The Sherm Feller Show was Boston's most lively evening show and many of us used to enjoy taking in the show at WEEI studios located on Tremont Street, Boston.

In the late forties, radio was still the prime source for information and entertainment for Bostonians. There were also enough farmers in the area for stations like WBZ and WNAC to include programs for farmers. WBZ featured at 6 a. m. "The New England Farmhouse", and WNAC scheduled at 6:15 a. m. "The Farm Journal". Running up against WNAC's "Journal" was "The Fisherman's News" on WHDH. WCOP was another radio station with an early morning program appealing to area farmers called, "Farm Market Facts".

Some of the popular radio programs during the late forties were: "Carnival of Music" with Fred B. Cole on WHDH at 10 a. m., my mother's favorite morning program. Running up against him was "Rapleff's Record Shop" on WNAC. At 1 p. m., "Matinee With Bob and Ray" proved popular with housewives.

For high schoolers with homework, they tuned into such programs as Bob Clayton's Boston Ballroom on WHDH or the 920 Club on WROL. The romantics, on the other hand, listened to Doris Day on WNAC, or WBZ's *soap* "Backstage Wife".

Because of so many programs, Boston radio station sales executives could easily pitch a program to advertisers to reach their potential market. If an advertiser wanted to reach men, they would pitch sports news which every station included in their line-up of programs such as Bump Hadley on WBZ or Jim Britt on WHDH.

As for kiddie programs, WNAC featured at 5:45 p. m. Tom Mix, and WCOP featured Sky King. Other kid programs were: Yukon Challenge on WCOP and Captain Midnight on WNAC.

In 1949 television was in its infancy. Bostonians affording television sets had a choice of 36 programs. WNAC-TV, Channel 7, began to telecast their programs at 5:28 p. m. with a two-minute preview of programs for the evening. WBZ-TV, Channel 4 flicked their "on" switch at 5 p. m., running a serial "These Are My Children". Both stations scheduled news and weather programs sponsored by two Boston banks. At 7:45 p. m., viewers could watch "The Shawmut Newsletter" on WNAC-TV, followed by the "Shawmut Weather Fotocast" at

7:55. At 6:30 p. m., WBZ-TV ran "Weather" sponsored by The First National Bank of Boston.

One of the most popular television shows at 6 p. m. was Bob Emery's "Small Fry Club" on WNAC-TV. Yes, Emery was originally on WNAC-TV and later moved his program to WBZ-TV.

The latter stopped transmitting pictures at 11:05 p. m., and the former at 12:16 a. m. both stations used to sign off with a listing of "Tomorrow's Programs".

Some of the top billing radio salesmen during the war years were: Roy Marks of WEEI, Nat Herman and Murray Travers both selling for WNAC and the station's Yankee Network.

The structure of the advertising agencies was less complicated than today's. For example, agencies did not have media buyers, creative or research directors. The account executives did the media buying and market research. Agencies employed copywriters and commercial artists, known today as graphic designers or art directors.

In 1943, Gus Saunders joined WNAC (Now WRKO) as a staff announcer and news anchor. Born in Italy, Gus, whose true name is Solimene, was one of the first Italian-Americans hired by the station. For young Saunders, a graduate of Harvard with a degree in economics, joining WNAC was heavy stuff. Let's say it was good luck. As you probably have read, when the war broke out, our government interned Japanese-Americans, and there were discussions in Washington about rounding-up Italian and German-Americans as well. It did not happen, thanks mainly to Judge Felix Forte working with organizations such as The Sons of Italy. Fortunately, we had some cool headed people in Washington who pointed out that Italian and German-Americans represented too large a percentage of the population; besides, they were considered loyal and trustworthy. To think, if Italian-Americans had been interned—where would you have put us all?—Gus Saunders would never have had the opportunity to carve out a distinguished career as a broadcaster and journalist.

I asked Harry Wheeler, one of the senior citizens of broadcast, to dig back into his memory cells to recall those turbulent years. Harry wasted no time recalling some of the goings-on in advertising and broadcast. Harry, who had passed the Bar and was practicing law, was also selling radio time for WORL and WCOP. According to this articulate man, many of Boston's radio stations used to sell program sponsorship as well as spot announcements. For example, Victor Coffee used to sponsor Fulton Lewis, Jr.. The agency handling Victor Coffee was John C. Dowd. The big spot buyers were Albany Carpets, NECCO Candies and First National Stores. Other big billing accounts advertising in newspapers and radio were: Whiting Milk, Andy Boy Broccoli and H.P. Hood.

Harry reminded me there were no rating services available to advertising agencies during those years. The only way a radio salesman proved the popularity of a program was measured by the station's mail pull. Radio salesmen used to haul mail bags around to advertising agencies dumping the contents on the top of the account executive's desk to prove they had listeners. One station that impressed advertising agencies by their mail-pull was WBZ. It pulled mail from the Boston area as well as from such states as Maryland, Colorado and Arizona. The station had and still has a powerful signal.

Some of the heavy users of radio was Badger & Browning which had the NECCO account. Working at the agency was Paul Provandie and Paul Hoag, both, after the war, launching their own agency. Larry Duane, who was also working with Badger handling the First National Store account, left the agency with the account in his back pocket and moving it to John C. Dowd.

Ingalls-Miniter was another Boston agency widely noted and recognized for specializing in radio advertising. Its major accounts were Whiting Milk and La Torraine Coffee.

At Chambers & Wiswell, Richard Montgomery Mason was the account executive handling Andy Boy Broccoli.

One of Harold Cabot & Company's big radio spenders was H. P. Hood. The milk company used to sponsor the E. B. Rideout Weather program across-the-board each morning at 7:55 on WEEI.

My favorite radio show while attending Boston English High was the Bob Perry "920 Club" on WORL which I listened to while doing my home work which always prompted my mother to ask, "How can you concentrate on your homework and listen to the radio at the same time?" What else is new! My report card was the answer—barely passable marks!

In 1948, the growth of Boston's broadcast industry prompted Nona Kirby, who was in the radio rep business, to organize an association made up of individuals working in broadcast. Her efforts resulted in the establishment of the Radio Executives Club of New England. Assisting her were Harry Wheeler, the local sales manager of WCOP, and Bill McGrath of WHDH.

With television coming into its own in New England, it was decided to change the name of the association to The Radio and TV Advertising Executives Club of New England. The new name proved to be a mouthful; so it was decided to shorten it to The Broadcast Executive Club. In 1968, its directors changed it to New England Broadcasting Association.

With the forties coming to an end, the beginning of the new decade proved fruitful for the many new radio stations springing up throughout the country. According to FCC records, as of August 1, 1950, there were 2,160 AM and 687 FM radio stations. Licensed television stations in 1950 totaled only 106. The following year, the FCC gave the go-ahead for an additional 1,945 television licenses, thus causing America to change drastically in just about every aspect of life.

Things truly would never be the same again.

Advertisements of the forties, which appeared in magazines and newspapers are now considered to be collector's items. There are stores specializing in selling many of the colorful ads created during the decade. The specialty shops/stores also stock many of the packaging of that period such as cocoa tins and labels used on orange crates. Yesteryear's advertising—memories of when advertising was beginning to become a profession.

It was said that you could easily judge the ideals of a nation by its advertisements. The advertisements of the forties were symbols of a nation which was beginning to enjoy new affordable products such as automobiles and fur coats. It was a time of prosperity. It's when we were dreamers of dreams!

My favorite column.

Chapter Thirteen

W ho would think back in the forties someday I would be firmly entrenched in the world of advertising as a copywriter, ad manager of a company, promotion director of a radio station and also as a columnist for *New England Business Journal* and then for *New England Ad Week*. Mind you, I worked on my columns as I was making my living as a principal of an advertising agency. I found time to write between servicing accounts, media meetings, creating advertising and marketing plans, etc. The columns helped to relax me—they became my wine.

Perhaps my life and time during the forties conditioned me in the sense I could juggle more than one thing at a time. As you previously read, my lifestyle during that decade was hardly a normal one. As they say, I had everything going at once. Nat Hentoff, the distinguished author/journalist, pretty much covered my "comings and goings" in an article he wrote about me for *Down Beat* Magazine. Here then are some highlights of the lengthy piece he did, which I believe will explain the nature of my character and more:

"Mr. Music Business—
The Eight Public Lives of Ray Barron

"A nationally known musician was relaxing between sets at Boston's *Hi-Hat*. One of his sidemen came over to ask perplexedly, 'Ever since I've been here, I hear the name, Ray Barron, whenever anything connected with music comes up. Who is the guy? Just what does he do?'

"The leader grinned. 'It's hard to know where to start. Sometimes I don't believe there's only one of him. He's a musician; he owns his own record company and has been a recording director for others; he's the personnel manager for several bands; he's a publicist, a disc-jockey, a jazz columnist and Boston correspondent for *Down Beat,* and he's a jazz concert promoter.'

"It *has* been difficult for music-minded New Englanders not to believe that by some amazing coincidence, there aren't eight different people—all named Ray Barron. This multi-faceted marvel, however, manages to combine at least eight full-time activities into one career, a career all the more remarkable since Ray is only twenty-seven years old.

"Ray began his all-encompassing musical life as a violinist at the age of thirteen. He switched to drums a year later, and at fifteen had his own band. The Barron band worked cafes, ballrooms, high school dances and attained a reputation that garnered it considerable praise in Boston newspapers. Ray meanwhile had been graduated from Boston English High School, the nation's oldest public school, and he went to earn a degree from Burdett College as well as the Conn School of Music, the Schillinger House and the George B. Stone School of Percussion.

"At twenty one, Ray organized a large dance band in Boston which played college dates, ballrooms, hotels and theaters, and it seemed that his future was assured as a bandleader. Restless Ray, though, felt that music alone was not sufficient for him as a means of communication. As a result, he joined the staff of the Neighborhood Publishers in 1947 and wrote a weekly column, *Melody and Harmony,* for newspapers in Cambridge, Somerville and East Boston. His articles quickly caused comment and reaction not only in the three cities, but also from various musical fans in Europe, who somehow had obtained copies of the column. A jazzophile in Oslo, Norway, instituted what was to have been a world-wide jazz union and appointed Ray the representative of the league in America.

"Those who knew Ray were certain his journalistic activities would inevitably expand as had his musical undertakings, and they were right. The 'Musicians" Bible, *Down Beat,* asked him to be their Boston representative in 1948, a post he has held since then. His major exclusive for the *Beat* was the sensational expose of the Johnny Bothwell orchestra and its connection with the *Look* Magazine Teen-Age Band of America. Ray's news sense saved a group of inexperienced youngsters from further exploitation and served notice that not all unscrupulous deals are accomplished with impunity. Ray was also the first critic in the country to review the Ralph Flanagan orchestra and his accurate appraisal was quoted by the trade press and disc-jockeys all over the country. Ray has had other notable articles in *Down Beat,* which have brought him mail from all parts of the world.

"During this period of reportorial activity, Ray was continuing his active musicianship. He drummed with Roy Eldridge, Hot Lips Page, Hal Singer and other combos. At jam sessions he not only played, but often promoted the concerts and was the first to present a modern jazz session on the North Shore at the 20th Century Cafe while president of the North Shore Jazz Society.

"Simultaneously, Ray was active in the establishment of several jazz centers in Boston. In 1948, he was responsible for helping to establish the *Down Beat* club as one of Boston's leading jazz niteries. A year later, when Julius Rosenberg opened the *Hi-Hat*, now nationally recognized as Boston's modern music center, Ray was an integral part of the policy making and publicity functions of the club.

"Ray's experience as a publicist has also included close association with Stan Kenton and Jazz at the Philharmonic during their New England tours. As a personal manager, he has been instrumental in the success of the Mickey Long Trio the Eccentrics, a fantastically versatile musical comedy trio, and has just begun active management of a group headed by the brilliant modern trumpeter, Red Rodney, the new combo of drummer Jack Parker and Rudy William's orchestra. Also under the Barron aegis are Al Vega, Paul Vignoli and Les Desmond. Ray, incidentally, includes as part of his managerial services an expert knowledge of accounting and tax problems.

"Having explored every other part of the music business, Ray went into the recording field, as a recording director. Now, as owner of Barron and Artistry records, Ray has direct facilities to further the careers of young musicians. While taking part in the record business, Ray also turned music publisher and opened his own Boston office to handle all of his interwoven activities.

"There was still one avenue of the record realm Ray had not yet entered, and this year he filled that hiatus, becoming a successful disc-jockey on Boston's WVOM, where he utilized his wide knowledge of all phases of music to create an original and informational program.

"Ray Barron has now participated in every conceivable form of musical activity in the New England area. The next step is a forward one to New York, where Ray will have greater opportunities to expend both his knowledge and energy in the furtherance of the vocations of the musicians whose adviser and manager he has become. In New York, Ray plans to advance his proteges by means of all the available media—radio, TV, recordings and night club dates. Although New England musicians regret seeing Ray leave, they expected that in time New England would be too small an arena for the man with eight lives.

"Recently Ray was saluted by Paul Masterson of CBS in Hollywood and by the magazine, *Billboard*, as 'Mr. Music Business of New England'. You can see how this title was, if anything, an understatement. It looks now as if 'Mr. Music Business of the United States' may conceivably come next. As we said at the beginning of this profile, Ray is only twenty seven."

Nat Hentoff

Once I existed.

Chapter Fourteen

W hy do I write, paint and make music? The fear of ano-
nymity—dying and being forgotten? Aren't most people more
afraid of being forgotten than of dying? So, I create, keep
diaries, and save countless documents to prove I once existed. It
was in recent years I discovered to have made some sort of
history in the music, art, and advertising profession. I did not
plan it that way. Still, I have fears of being forgotten.

Individuals go through life probing and searching for the
meaning of life. Some spend their lifetime trying to achieve
monetary success; others strive to become leaders of their business or professions. . .to be number one. Many enjoy sharing
their lives with others, to help or to inspire them. A good
example of one who sacrificed part of his life to help others was
Albert Schweitzer, a doctor, theologian, philosopher and musician—his two volume work on Bach (Branden Press) is a
classic.

I discovered him in 1949 while listening to a recording of
one of his lectures on Johann W. Goethe. In listening to
Schweizter's voice, I sensed he was a rare human being. So I
embarked on a quest to learn more about this man, who was
sharing his life with the poor and sick in Africa. Through the
years, I collected his books, those written by others about him,
and the recordings of Schweitzer playing the organ, his favorite
composer being Johann Sebastian Bach.

In 1971, thanks to Bill Hahn, director of community affairs of WNAC-TV—now WNEV-TV, I was allowed to videotape a thirty-second message appealing for support of the Albert Schweizter Friendship House and Library in Great Barrington, Massachusetts.

On June 27, 1971, I was invited by Erica Anderson, director of the House, to attend a dedication ceremony for the newly completed facility. With my wife, Marilyn, we joined others who journeyed to Great Barrington for the dedication. There I had another memorable experience of life, meeting Pablo Casals, Norman Cousins, Dr. Schweizter's daughter Rhena, and many others who loved and respected Schweizter. It was a beautiful sunny day in the Berkshires—a beautiful day of my life. Reverence for life became more important to me.

In the following pages, I'd like to share with you some of my thoughts on topical issues, beginning with the one that appeared in *New England Ad Week* in 1984. The article pretty much covers my life and times as a columnist and my love for writing. I authored columns for close to eight years. When the publication was sold, I inherited a young, new editor, and soon discovered we were not compatible. So, I took a walk to *Ad East*, another trade publication.

As a columnist, I'm used to asking questions. But for once, I am going to devote my entire column to answer yours.

For years, you see, you've been asking, how I find time to write, where I get my information, what the life of a columnist is really like.

Moreover, many of the people I am particularly close to, report they are often asked what I'm really like.

OK, here it is, once and for all, a complete behind-the-scene look at yours truly. Or, as that famous, Chicago-based broadcast journalist, Paul Harvey would say: "And now. . .the rest of the story."

This is my 125th column for *New England Ad Week*. What's more, I am now launching my sixth year with this widely-read publication. It hasn't been all that easy. Bud Tominey, publisher of NEAW and Charles Jackson, editor, have saved me from potential physical assaults as well as law suits by editing carefully some of the stuff I submitted for publication. And so, I add this edition to the collection of countless columns not only for NEAW, but for *Down Beat*, Times Publications, Tribune Publications, New England Business Journal, etc..

My first venture into journalism was at the age of 12 when I launched a two-page newspaper using an antique hand-press. My paper, *The Tattletale* survived for three weeks. I still have a copy.

At the end of World War II, my commanding officer asked me to help put together the battle history of our unit. So, in a small room in Munich, West Germany, using a German typewriter, I relived the war.

In 1947, I had my first weekly column published by Times Publications, a group of weeklies. The column was called *Melody and Harmony*. Soon after, I began to cover New England for *Down Beat* Magazine. At last writing for an internationally recognized publication—heavy stuff for an admitted illiterate!

Last year, I accepted an offer from the *Boston Herald* to author a weekly column, which, of course, added more tear-sheets to my files. When I'm not writing about the industry, I write about my travels. A recent article about Ireland made the rounds of greater Boston newspapers, producing touching letters from Irish-American readers.

As a columnist (off and on) for over 37 years, I have had the opportunity to meet a wide variety of prominent and not-so-prominent individuals. With ease, I can drop names of politicians, poets, artists, musicians, actors, tycoons. What's more, some of those individuals either loved or despised me. George Higgins, author-columnist, once took off on me. Why, even Christopher Lyndon, who interviewed me for the *Boston Globe* wasn't too polite in describing me. So it goes!

In an Associated Press feature story, I was described as follows: "He's billed as *The Outrageous Ray Barron*, a dynamo with a wild head of hair and a knack for infuriating advertising and media people. Ray Barron is a celebrity within his industry and a self-professed prophet among reluctant disciples who cower from his speeches and columns." Not so!

What do my readers enjoy the most? When I drop into my columns, "What some People Look Like." Some of these people reacted with anger and some accepted my descriptions of them calmly.

Columnists get wined and dined, receive invitations to premieres, press parties, orgies, etc. I rarely take notes, only because I have good memory cells in my head. I enjoy meeting people because they are interesting to me. The only bores are those who walk up to me trying to degrade me.

To date, I have had the opportunity to appear as guest speaker at Ad Club luncheons or dinners throughout New England and in Albany, New York. Some of my speaking engagements bombed; others were well received. Perhaps the most enjoyable of all engagements were at the colleges and universities.

One draw back as a columnist: too many job seekers ask me for advice or job leads. I receive an average of 10 calls per week from individuals asking me to meet with them. I have also received numerous calls from individuals working in the advertising and broadcast industry asking for advice.

Some years ago, I used to lunch with George Frazier (one of my idols) who, like myself, used to write for *Down Beat* Magazine. George told me stories about how people reacted to his columns in *The Boston Herald*. In one column, George insinuated a local politician had ties with the *Mafia* in Sicily, and his life was threatened. I asked George if he was frightened. "Ray, it's all part of the job. Every profession has its hazards and dangers. You learn how to live with them."

I have two file cabinets housing letters from readers dating back to 1947. I cherish them. My daughters Robyn and Karen enjoy reading some of those letters, including those savaging me. The letters which annoy me are from anonymous authors—cowards that call me *kike, fag-lover, or stinking wop*!

When I'm not writing, I oil paint pastoral scenes. My favorite subjects are autumn and winter scenes. Painting offers me the opportunity to explore the world of tranquility. If I'm not writing or painting, I make music. I sit at the organ or at the piano and play my heart out. Music has always been important to me. I have composed some stuff which could only be played by Santana, Moody Blues or ELO.

My wine? Books!

I read and collect autobiographies, biographies, history and art books. I'm proud of my library which goes back to my high school years.

Nancy Ingersoll, who has been associated with me for many years, continuously asks: "What! Another column to go out?"

"Yes Nancy, another column of *useless* information."

Of all my columns, the ones I enjoyed the most were for *New England Ad Week*. In order to establish their impact, I asked Charles Jackson, its editor, for his comments:

"To understand Ray Barron's contributions to *New England Ad Week* it is important to comprehend the context in which Ray's association with NEAW was born and developed. It was founded in 1964 by Thomas J. Tierney, who had a long association with the Boston Ad club as publisher of *Ad News*, a newsletter for the club with local community circulation. Tierney was aware of the early success of regional trade publications for advertising in Los Angeles and New York which were soon followed by a similar start-up in Chicago. Following a disagreement with the management of the Boston Ad Club, Tierney decided to launch *New England Ad Week*.

"In late 1967, Tierney sold his company (whose principal product was a regional trade publication called *New England Printer an Lithographer*, including *New England Ad Week* to Francis J. Tominey, who had been Tierney's sales manager and assistant general manager since 1946. I had become editor (the first full time editor of New England Ad Week) in 1966, 18 months after the publication was launched.

"NEAW developed as an extremely conservative publication reflecting its non-controversial antecedent of a club newsletter plus the personal philosophy of its new owner, Francis J. Tominey. In fairness, NEAW also reflected the spirit of business journalism of the late sixties and early seventies: 'Don't rock the boat' and 'If you can't say anything nice, don't say anything at all.'

"But a new spirit of business journalism was emerging which treated news business in the same manner as news of politics and sports. In part because NEAW management was reluctant to change its ideas that most business activities were nobody's business except those directly involved and that the trade press, and indeed the general press, existed only to report the 'good news' and support the powers of the establishment (whatever that might be), a new regional New England advertising publication was founded in March, 1970. The monthly was called *Ad East*, billing itself as a commentary, and supporting a philosophy of advocacy and investigative journalism.

"In the competition with *Ad East* during the early and mid-seventies, NEAW survived and eked out a living for those involved with it even during the severe recession which decimated the publishing business in 1972-74. But an objective observer would conclude that NEAW failed to gain the princi-

pal positioning as the leader publication for the business inter-
ests it served during that time period. *Ad East* set the tone, was
much talked about whenever it appeared, and NEAW was
generally considered as a bland product being produced by
good guys.

"As editor, I adapted to the situation I could not change, but
underneath harbored a desire to make the publication more
vital to the community it served. I sought ways to enliven
NEAW without getting shot down by the timidity of the
management.

"Enter Ray Barron. Among the many publications which
crossed my desk as editor of NEAW in the mid-seventies was
one called *New England Business Journal*. I noted to myself that I
always took the time to at least survey a column in that publication by one Ray Barron, an advertising agency principal of
whom I had heard but never met. Then in 1978, I believe, at
some holiday function, I recall meeting Barron and comment-
ing to him that I always used to read his column in the *Journal*,
which had gone under by this time. Ray's immediate response
to me was, 'Would you like me to write for you (meaning
NEAW)?' I gulped and said, 'Sure, send one in and I'll try it
out as a pilot.' I knew Ray's easy, breezy style with its gossipy
emphasis on people would be a departure from the normal
heaviness of NEAW editorial product, but I was not at all
certain that I could have it incorporated into the publication
without upsetting the applecart of management.

"When the column arrived, I simply ran it. I had learned
that with Mr. Tominey the best policy was often just to act;
wait for the sputter and fumes to die down; and then knowing
that what Mr. Tominey feared most was confrontation, he
would generally accede to the condition that had been changed
without his prior approval.

"Ray's column, which he tagged 'The 11 O'Clock News',
was indeed a departure from the NEAW norm. Ray's patter

was based in part on people (who or what they looked like; where they were moving) and in part on news items, particularly those which held a gossipy interest such as who's going out of business and who's going to win or lose business. The latter did not always appear in print as the censorship was applied with a strong hand by NEAW management if the slightest hint of negativism toward any individual could be surmised.

"I recall the day when I understood that Ray Barron's column in NEAW was becoming a factor in changing the perception of our publication from that of a dowdy old lady to at least that of a world-wise matron. It was at a cocktail party being held by the Harold Cabot advertising agency. As I stood there in the middle of a large room in some bank building in downtown Boston sipping my cocktail with the chief executive of Cabot, Paul McDermott walked into the room, and Jim Summers, president of Cabot, spotting him across the way, called out, 'Paul McDermott, you do look like a Carvel ice cream salesman.' I knew then that if the president of a large advertising agency was reading and then *remembering* Ray Barron's often off-the-wall remarks, Ray Barron was indeed serving an important function in making NEAW a more readable and pertinent publication.

"Ray Barron continued to write of NEAW until the publication was sold to A.S.M. Publications in 1986. He became part of the character of the journal and aided in changing its image and positioning to the point where it became the leading publication in its region for advertising and communications. He was NEAW's steam valve, speaking that which we could not (or would not) say elsewhere in the magazine.

"He was controversial. He had his foes, but he also had his friends and a loyal following who frequently made known to this editor their passion for his prose. Those who knew Ray agreed: beneath the bombastic veneer and the sarcastic facade was a puppy dog. . .loyal to his friends and longing for their approval.

"The best relationships are those which serve the interest of all parties concerned equally well. Ray Barron was an asset who helped change the perception of NEAW and transform it into the valuable property it became in the 1980s."

Art

I first discovered art in churches at an early age—stained glass windows, sculptures of saints and religious murals.

My deep interest and knowledge about art (all styles and periods) can be attributed to my visiting museums, art galleries and reading countless art periodicals from around the world. What's more, I invested money in books about art and artists.

My home, according to some people, is like a museum or an art gallery. I have paintings, sculptures and some of my own oils covering our walls through the house—including the bathrooms!

Years ago, J. W. S. Cox, one of America's most renown water colorists and late president of the New England School of Art, urged me to lecture at the school on how to market art, how to open an art gallery, how to promote art, etc.. So for 15 years, I worked with fine art and graphic design majors and enlightened them about the business and art world. I have also been a guest speaker at Massachusetts College of Art, Gloucester Art Academy and Museum School of Art.

One of the "art promotions" I am proud of is when, some years ago, I helped to introduce "art-in-the-subways". It was covered by the press, and the artists who participated in my project received valuable publicity and credits.

Staging "one-man" shows was challenging. I staged one of Paul Szep's first (political) art shows at Gallery 28 on Newbury Street, Boston. I have also staged shows for John Hahn,

Michael Karas and Ralph Fasanella. One show which attracted hundreds of art lovers was *Illuminations*, at the Pacifico Gallies for 12 young artists. A few years ago, I put together a show at the Art Gallery of Boston called *"An Art Attack"*, also well attended. Perhaps my biggest thrill was to be commended by Betty Chamberlin of *American Artists* Magazine for helping artists to market their art.

One internationally famous artist I have been close to is Ralph Fasanella of New York, hailed as an artist at the level of Grandma Moses. Fasanella has appeared on countless TV shows; the BBC shot a documentary film on him; a book, *Fasanella's World,* continues as a perennial seller. His art is found in museums throughout the world. A colorful character, Ralph was a member of the Lincoln Brigade during the Spanish Civil War and knew Papa Hemingway. I've spent countless hours with him in New York and in Boston. Ralph has asked me to write a book about his life and times as a political activist and artist. Perhaps I'll tackle it in the autumn years of my life.

One of my favorite artists is Amedeo Modigliani, an Italian Jew. Years ago, *The Boston Globe* ran a feature story about my great passion for Modigliani's art. I have a large collection of his (reproductions) pictures and a few of his sculptures. I became an expert on Modigliani and own every book published about this gifted artist. I visited Pierre Lachaisse Cemetery in Paris to place flowers on his resting place. Close by his grave is that of Gertrude Stein and Alice Toklas, where of course, I have also placed flowers.

The periods I find exciting: the Bauhaus, Symbolists, Post Impressionism and the Abstract Impressionist period. Frankly, I love any style or art period which turns me on.

Do I own any art of importance? I own a Buffet, a Dufy, paintings of Karas, original prints by Hahn and Fasanella, a J. W. S. Cox watercolor, a Jack Coughlin print of James Joyce, and much, much more.

One of my favorite museums is located in the Southern part of France, the Maeght Museum. When I ventured to the Cannes Film Festival, I spent one day at the Maeght. Not many tourists are aware of this beautiful museum, which houses indoor and outdoor art created by Chagall, Picasso, Giacommetti, and other creative geniuses of the recent past.

My love for art inspired me to organize and launch the Nahant Arts Association. Each year, we draw hundreds of people to the outdoor festival that's held over the Memorial Day weekend. Needless to say, I'm proud of being referred to as the founding father of the association.

Through the years, various associations have asked me to serve as judge. One year, the Swampscott Art Association called me to judge entries for their annual show, and discovered Swampscott is loaded with great artists. It was one of the most difficult shows I ever judged.

My favorite art association? The North Shore Art Association, located in East Gloucester. Some of America's greatest artists are members of this prestigious association. I also attended shows sponsored by the Rockport Art Association. My favorite Rockport artist is Don Stone, who lives and paints in Maine. I enjoy attending art shows throughout New England and in New York. My love for art and artists has been of great inspiration and helps to make life a bit more poetic and romantic. So it goes.

I have often wondered if I inherited my love for art from Barisano di Trani, a thirteen century artist and sculptor of the cathedral bronze doors of Trani, of Ravello and of Monreale, Italy. The late author-artist Samuel Chamberlain, photographed the beautiful Barisano di Trani bronze doors and gifted me with a large print of the doors of Ravello. Yes, my family roots originated in Trani, Italy, where 150,000 Italian Jews lived and worked since the 11th century.

Art, like music and literature, have always dominated my home. My daughters, Karen and Robyn have, of course, been influenced by the environment of our home. I can proudly state that they both know the difference between Renaissance and Bauhaus art. Before reaching the ages of three and four (they are fourteen months apart), they could rattle off names of artists with ease. As for Marilyn, my wife, she's also into art. Back thirty years, she did a sculpture of my head, which compliments me. Marilyn has also created collages, but her artistic expression is in floral arrangements. She has, through the years, won many blue and red ribbons for some of her floral arrangements.

Let me leave you with something to talk about at your next cocktail party, to prove you know something about art. The statue of Rodin that has come to be known as *The Thinker* was not meant to be a portrait of a man in thought but a portrait of Dante, the poet.

Music

My first musical instrument was the violin at the age of 13. After three months of lessons, I switched to drums and played for the local American Legion Post drum and bugle corps. On entering English High School, I switched to a full set of drums I purchased on time payments at a pawn shop in Boston's South End. My mother threatened to toss me out of the house on learning I had purchased the set. "The neighbors will go crazy!" And they did!

I organized a small orchestra—all kids like myself, and we tried hard to make musical sense rehearsing in the basement of my house.

My first professional job was at the age of fifteen, playing at a roadside cafe, the "Lucky Stop Cafe", on Beachmont Road in Orient Heights. Our wages amounted to a few bucks each, plus free orange pop or gingerale. After three weekends, we were fired—people couldn't dance to our music.

By age seventeen, "Ray Barron and His Orchestra" had made the rounds of ballrooms, halls, high school gyms, etc.. We also picked up wedding gigs. I'll never forget some weddings because of the many fights between the bride and the groom's families.

World War II broke out as Ray Barron and His Orchestra was just beginning to mature and swing, like some of the other big bands such as Glenn Miller, Benny Goodman and Artie Shaw. The war brought my career to a halt! I was one of the first eighteen year olds to be drafted into the U.S. Army. So off I went to Camp Swift, Texas, to join the 97th Infantry Division leaving behind my drums, musical arrangements and lots of great memories.

At Camp Swift, I attended jazz concerts which the USO booked for the "colored soldiers". Yes, my dear friends, it was a segregated army. I made my way to the "colored theatre" to enjoy listening to some great jazz artists. I was one of the few "offays" in attendance—the rest being white officers. More than once I was asked what I was doing in the "colored section".

From Texas to England to prepare for the invasion of France. While in England, I "sat-in" with British dance bands and met, at one of the dances, a lovely blond British girl who came close to being my wife. Well, that's another story.

After the war, back home to college and the Ray Barron Band again. More ballrooms, hotels, theatres, college proms, Dartmouth Ice Carnival, USO tour and other memorable bookings. Soon, a possible recording contract! We were swinging. Life was exciting—radio remotes and seeing the name "Ray Barron and His Orchestra" up on the marquee, newspapers and mentions on radio. I disbanded the orchestra in 1950. I made the decision after an engagement at the Charleshurst Ballroom,

Salem Willows. I can still remember that evening when I announced to the guys this would be our last gig. Why? Because it was wearing me down. Perhaps it was also because I was leaning more toward playing jazz with small groups—freedom from orchestral regimentation.

My last professional job as a musician was at the posh Casa Madrid in West Yarmouth, Cape Cod, a supper club, and I was a member of the house band. We played floor shows and for dancing seven nights a week. It was a long summer of working nights, dating after hours and meeting many interesting people. The Cape was in those years "restricted", meaning Jews were not welcomed. One evening, while finishing up, we headed for Hyannis to the Mayflower for a snack. On our way out, a group of young men shouted at us, "Hey! Kikes! Go back where you came from!" Musicians do not engage in brawls. We just walked away in disbelief.

My love for contemporary jazz prompted me to stage weekly concerts, which I presented at place like *The Down Beat Club* and finally at the Hi-Hat, which became known as Boston's leading jazz spot. And so "Ray Barron Presents" was included in all of the advertising. It was at the *Hi-Hat* where I first met Herb Frank, who had an ad agency and handled the accounts and publicity of both clubs.

At the *Hi-Hat* I met some of the jazz greats of America, such as Billie Holliday, Count Basie, Eroll Garner, Buddy Rich and many others. We socialized after hours at the Pioneer Club, an all-night private club.

Some of the individuals and groups I sat-in with as a drummer: Roy Eldridge, Howard McGhee, Oscar Pettiford and many, many others. Biggest thrill was when Buddy Rich asked me to take over his drums for an hour. Imagine, one of my idols allowing me to sit in with his all-star group. I also "sat-in" with Count Basie, Stan Getz, Buddy De Franco and other illustrious jazz musicians. Frankly, I never considered myself a great drummer, even though I did study with Harry Stone and took lessons with Charles Smith of the Boston Symphony Orchestra.

From Boston to New York City! I lived and worked in New York City for about four years. New York was one big ball for the young Ray Barron, who at that time did not sport a pear shape body. I loved my women and some loved me, too. I dated vocalists, exotic dancers and some "squares". My apartment was known as the "tender trap".

There I became known as a personal manager of jazz musicians and vocalists such as Terry Gibbs, Lee Konitz, Zoot Sims, Red Rodney, Teddy Charles and Marty Napoleon. I was instrumental in getting Marty to work with Louis Armstrong and I still have letters from Marty, who used to write while traveling with Armstrong about some of his experiences with the band. Marty, a pianist, was the only white member of the group and it was a *Crow Jim* (reverse discrimination).

Also in New York, I was instrumental in landing recording contracts for some of my stable of jazz musicians. One track on an LP featuring Red Rodney was named after me, *The Baron*.

My life and time in the world of music would require at least two hundred more pages, just on my experience with drug addicted and starving musicians, has-been movie stars, pimps, junkies, the "fuzz", and being run out of Harrisburg, Pennsylvania.

Hillbilly

After having written about jazz, I found myself praising hillbilly music. I was more or less obligated to pour my heart out over it for the souvenir book of The New England Hillbilly Jamboree held at the Boston Garden in 1953. When I wrote the article, I was employed at WCOP radio in Boston as promotion and publicity director. At that time, the station was programming hillbilly music.

On writing "Mr. and Miss England Go Hillbilly", I felt like a traitor. You see, I never cared for hillbilly, and to place it up with jazz was painful. Ironically, though struggling to write about it, I tried to convince myself that hillbilly music, perhaps, wasn't all that bad. The boss, Roy Whisnand, general manager of WCOP, liked what I wrote, and that's all that mattered. Today, hillbilly music is called 'country and western". Here's the piece:

"Mr. and Miss New England Go Hillbilly

"What's come over people in New England? Nothing much except that hillbilly music is in the air and it agrees with them very much. The present hillbilly craze in N. E. has everybody wondering how it all started. It actually took exactly three steady hours of hillbilly music a day over one of the local radio stations. From three hours a day, hillbilly music was soon a newly-discovered style of music for New Englanders. Be-bop music never found a home in Boston, but hillbilly music did with hardly much effort or force. This all started back in the early part of 1952.

"Hillbilly jamboree are taking place all over New England. Even a network has been formed by eight radio stations thus assuring full coverage of all the New England states. No matter where you go you're sure to hear hillbilly music.

"The history of American music lists only two types of true American music—jazz and hillbilly. Foreigners refer to American music as jazz or hillbilly. It was then only natural that hillbilly music was easily accepted and loved by historic New England since history states that New England is the birth place of America and if it is American, it is New England.

"The best way to define hillbilly is that it represents every-day living set to music. It tells stories of work, of relaxed living or perhaps suffering; it tells about happiness and also about sadness. Unlike popular music, hillbilly tunes are much more flexible. The average popular song is usually based upon three or four subjects—love, stars, moon, and more love! Hillbilly music has no set pattern or subject. The composer bases his theme on complete inspiration. We'll admit that once in a while you'll hear a so-called idiotic tune, but compared to the popular music of the day, which involves electronics and trick recordings, gimmicks, etc., hillbilly music has stuck close to simple and plain music.

"As for the persons responsible for making hillbilly music popular in Boston, it took a combination of disc-jockies, cafes, record shops and the public's acceptance. The average lovers of hillbilly music have as their idol such names as Pee Wee King, Hank Snow, Grandpa Jones, Carl Smith, Hawkshaw Hawkins, etc. Like the popular music lovers who idolize Perry Como, Eddie Fischer, Frank Sinatra, etc., the hillbilly stars have also found their way into the hearts and minds of millions of lovers of their talents. New Englanders have turned out every time one of their idols made a personal appearance. Like Sinatra, Hank Snow was mobbed and asked for his autograph.

"No matter which way you look at it, hillbilly music is here to stay in New England. Every day a new discoverer of hillbilly art makes himself known by either rushing to a local record shop, requesting hillbilly records or by attending one of the many hillbilly jamborees and barn dances taking place all over the city and state."

Chapter Fifteen

I was 23 years old when I began to author columns about the world of music for the *East Boston Times*. I suggested to the publishers they needed a column about what was happening in music and more. Fortunately, one of the owners, Sal Tarbi, a musician, agreed to the idea—he would later play a one-week gig for my big band at the Rollaway Ballroom in Revere. He was a good bass player but I sensed his mind was more into the newspaper business than in plucking the strings of a bass fiddle.

I used to knock out my weekly columns, "Melody and Harmony" on an old Underwood typewriter in my bedroom. More than once, my mother would walk into my bedroom asking what I was writing about, and did I have to type so heavy? And so I added another activity and responsibility to my life. . . attending college, fronting a big band, and hustling for gigs. The *East Boston Times,* which was also publishing a Cambridge and Somerville weekly, decided to run my column in both publications. I was proud in being read by more people. I began to receive letters from readers asking questions about the big bands or jazz musicians: encouraging and inspiring.

Writing for *Down Beat* magazine was heady stuff for me! I began to read the publication in 1939 while attending Boston English High. It was the musicians's bible. One of my favorite *Down Beat* writers was George Frazier, who covered the Boston scene. Who was to think that some day this dummy would be following in his footsteps—writing for *Down Beat* and eventually getting to meet him and have some lively luncheons with him.

In 1947, in one of my "Melody and Harmony" columns, I covered Stan Kenton's band, which was appearing at Boston's RKO theatre on Washington Street. I went back stage to meet Kenton and some of the members of the band. I told Kenton how I enjoyed his "Progressive Jazz" music. Naturally, my column contained nothing but praises for Stan Kenton the man who started a civil war in the world of music. In 1942, Kenton's band appeared in Boston and George Frazier reported in *Down Beat:* "I'm very much afraid that the Stan Kenton band is going to be the great devastating success its admirers predicted it would be and I'm afraid too, that there's nothing to be done about it." George was hooked on Kenton in 1942 while I got hooked in 1947!

Anyway, what follows are sample columns.

I can still recall the day I sat to write about Glenn Miller. As I began to type away, in the background spinning on my portable phonograph was Miller's theme song, *Moonlight Serenade.* The piece, highly praised by the publisher of *The East Boston Times,* dates back to Thursday, December 4, 1947:

On December 15 it will be three years that one of America's best loved bandleaders has departed. When the familiar strains of *Moonlight Serenade* come over the radio, or are played by bands on the stage, or when you hum it, the first thought you have is Glenn Miller and the terrific band he had. It shouldn't be hard to recall some of the tunes that Americans listened to; and it wouldn't be hard to imagine you're listening to a band that sounds like an organ on sweet tunes. Perhaps more can be added about the distinct style the Miller band had. When it comes to band reminiscing, the Glenn Miller band is the first. Thinking of this band puts you right "in the mood".

On December 15, 1944 at Twin Woods Farm RAF Mosquito Base, England, a single engine Norseman C-64, an all metal plane equipped with one-way radio, fixed landing gear, awaited its passengers. This was the plane that had a reputation for treachery in bad weather. And this was the plane that would mysteriously disappear with its human cargo. It was close to two o'clock in the afternoon when the plane roared down the runway and the massive engines pulled it up into the unknown spaces. In the plane was Major Glenn Miller, who was on his way to Paris to have accomodations made for his band which was to follow. Many versions have been made about the trip. Some claim it was an authorized trip and others just keep making up stories. When the plane left the runway, Miller left musicdom. For days no word was received in Paris as to the whereabouts of Glenn Miller. Finally, on Christmas morning, members of the Miller band gathered in the empty Olympia Theatre to hear the sad news.

It was Lt. Haynes, orchestra manager, who mumbled out to the men that their Commanding Officer had officially been declared "missing in flight". This tragic news found its way all over Europe where Yanks were fighting. Major Glenn Miller had made us Americans feel at home in a foreign country. No more could be said about his flight into the sky which would end up tragically. He was "missing" and missed by millions throughout the world. 'Till V-E Day, music by the American Band of the A. E. F., found its way through flak, bombs, shells, etc., under the direction of Sgt. Ray McKinley and Sgt. Jerry Grey, a native of East Boston. The music that Glenn Miller made famous was continuing. The opening theme was still *Moonlight Serenade* but the soft voice of Glenn Miller wasn't there to open the program. Thus one of America's top leaders left musicdom with countless tunes in which to remember him by. Also to be remembered for his part in establishing American music firmly. Many musicians who have played for Glenn can remember him as a good guy to play for. He was the man responsible for encouragement to a few of his young musicians who moved into musicdom with their own bands. Each of them made the grade. (Hal McIntyre, Claude Thornhill and Charlie Spivack.) It was also Glenn who pushed Tex Beneke into the hearts of music lovers. (Glenn gave Beneke the name of "Tex".) He was highly respected for his keen interest he took in his sidemen.

Well, here it is in 1947 and it's three years without Glenn Miller. But, the last three years he has not been forgotten and for years to come his name will live in musicdom. Every day you're sure to hear the Miller name mentioned on disc shows, etc.. Many bands throughout the country make it a must to play Glenn Miller arrangements. Memorial sets have been played and tunes dedicated to him. I think it will be a long time before America will forget the Glenn Miller name. December fifteenth will be observed as *Moonlight Serenade Day* by countless musicians and fans.

On April 21, 1950, *Down Beat* published one of my favorite review on the newly formed Ralph Flanagan band. Here it is:

Boston—The newly organized Ralph Flanagan band made its debut at the King Phillip ballroom here on March 15. Some 2,000 persons packed the dancery for the opener which had only a cold New England night as a hindrance. And boyish-looking Flanagan didn't disappoint those who crowded around to hear the leader's well-uniformed band. The applause captured Flanagan to a point that left him speechless.

This same reception continued all evening, despite the frequent repetition of tunes.

Flanagan has no exploding personality, but his meek manner seems to click with the authograph seekers and well-wishers.

Majority Satisfied—The majority of the ballroom operators present were well satisfied with the reception tendered the new band, but other ops, like Roy Gill, who operates the largest dancery in New England, didn't find the crew any different or stimulating and didn't think it would revive the band industry. Gill's wife, however, made a note to buy Glenn Miller-styled stock arrangements for their house band.

Flanagan featured no names of any drawing value besides vocalists Harry Prime and Evelyn Joyce. Prime and Miss Joyce handled the few vocal arrangements that are well scattered through the library. That this was Miss Joyce's first public appearance was hard to believe, due to the poise she maintained all evening.

Criticism—Local band leaders who were on hand to pass judgement on the new band, mentioned spots which the band couldn't play due to monotonous style, lack of personality and showmanship, etc.. They also agreed that the trumpet section was pretty weak, and that Flanagan should either play more piano or hire a piano man.

Flanagan personnel: trumpets-Ralph Scaffide, Knobby Lee and Art Depew; trombones-Herb Spitalny, Phil Giacobbe, Blaise Powers; saxes-Joe Soldo, Red Press, Irving Hafter, George Benham, and Joe Walsh; rhythm-Tom O'Neill, bass, Sidney Bulkin, drums, and Flanagan, piano; vocals-Evelyn Joyce and Harry Prime.

Epilogue

The advertising industry has been continuously damned. But this isn't anything new. The damnation of advertising in America began in 1784 when it first began to appear in daily newspapers in New York, Philadelphia, and Boston. Advertising also came under attack in England in 1759 by no less than Dr. Samuel Johnson, who took to task the practitioners of advertising for "playing too wantonly with our passions." Today advertising is constantly assaulted as being sexist, obnoxious, and at times misleading. Nevertheless, the advertising industry continues to survive and thrive.

The image of the people working in advertising has also been a problem. Poll after poll proved people working in advertsising are rated no better than used car salesmen. Continuous efforts have been made by industry associations to better the image of our people and of advertising itself. Their effots are laudable.

With so much negativism, one wonders why anyone would want to be in the business. The answers vary. Some find it an exciting profession. Others will say they enjoy working in a creative environment. Others will claim that advertising pays well. Whatever the reasons, it appealed to me because, like jazz, advertising represents freedom from regimentation.

I have constantly been asked if I had any regrets for getting into the advertising profession. No! You see, the advertising business became a funnel for my love of art, music, writing and people. What's more, the world of advertising is fun, exciting—never boring. As you have read, I led a highly diversified life during the forties and it hasn't changed much since then.

Well, say what you want about the advertising profession, but just remember this—the people working in the industry are colorful, interesting and extremely bright.

One request, should you meet my mother, please don't tell her I'm in the advertising business—she still thinks I'm the piano player in a bordello.

The Forties
When We Were Dreamers of Dreams

Ray Barron as a bandleader, 1947.

Ray Barron and His Orchestra (1947) Rollaway Ballroom, Revere, MA.

Ray Barron with his first set of drums.

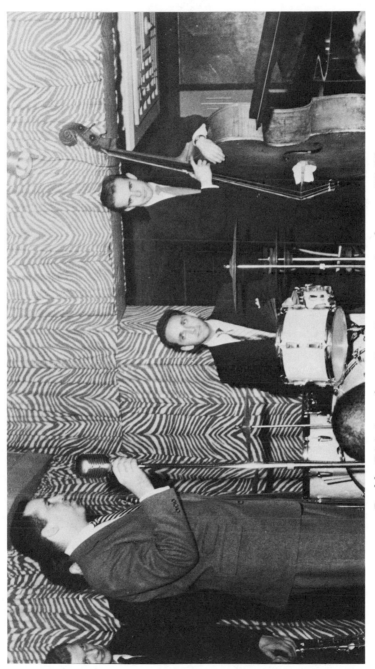

Buddy Rich introduces Ray Barron at the drums. Hi-Hat Club, Boston, MA, 1950.

Fallowfield, England, 1944.

Hi-Hat Club, Boston, 1949. Left to right: Joe Roland, Howard McGhee, Count Basie, Oscar Pettiford, Ray Barron, Dave Coleman and Stan Getz.

Roy Eldridge's autographed photo.

Appearing at the RKO Boston on-stage in 1942 was Harry Howard's "Beachcombers"—a musical revue. (*Boston Record-American*)

Carmen Miranda songstress and film star was the rage of the nation in 1943. Miranda, who stood 5'2" and weighed but 98 pounds, was noted for being "top heavy."

Tremont Street, Boston. Photograph was taken on May 28, 1942. Walt Disney's *Fantasia* was running at the RKO Keith Memorial Theatre. Many of the cars pictured here are today's costly antiques!

On May 8, 1945, Boston's newspaper celebrated the announcement of victory in Europe. Paper showers from buildings on either side of Washington Street. All traffic was halted and most downtown stores declared a holiday. (*Herald*)

On of the highlights of The Electric Show held in Boston on Aril 7, 1948 was Stewart-Warner's exhibit of a "videorama" television set. The exhibitor invited Louise Morgan of WNAC to pose for a publicity shot. (Lenscraft Studios)

FOR HAPPY HUSBANDS—WISE WIVES SERVE THE NEW

MAXWELL HOUSE
NOW 55% RICHER

IN EXTRA-FLAVOR COFFEES!

MORE OF THAT GRAND MAXWELL HOUSE, DEAR! COFFEE AS RICH AND DELICIOUS AS THIS CALLS FOR ANOTHER CUP!

New flavor, new richness added to the exclusive Maxwell House blend ... here's how we did it

In the forties, it was fashionable to cater to the man of the house—making him happy. This is typical of the ads of a wife performing her duties, waiting on her husband. Note the copy above the headline: For Happy Husbands—Wise Wives Serve The New. . .

MAXWELL HOUSE HAS ALWAYS BEEN GRAND...BUT NOW IT'S EVEN BETTER!

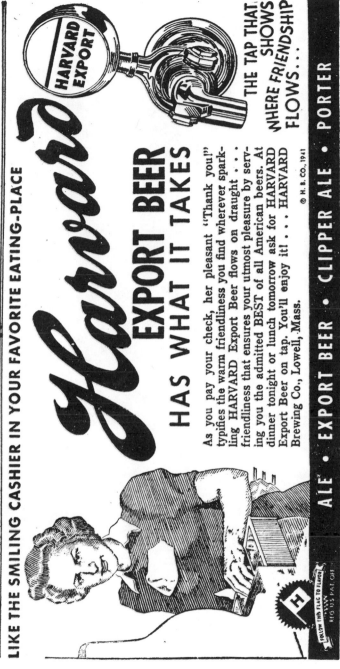

This advertisement ran in March, 1941 promoting "export beer," a specialty of Harvard Brewing Company, Lowell, MA. No clue is given as to where the beer was exported to. Harvard Brewing was another much sought after account by local advertising agencies.

says *Patsy* to *Pat*

Here's the
real smoker's cigarette
...the top o' good smoking
for smokers like us

Using movie stars to endorse products was becoming fashionable in the forties. Chesterfield featured in this ad Pat O'Brien, a popular screen star during that period. The young lady offering O'Brien a cigarette is Patsy Garrett, who was one of the singing stars of Fred Waring's radio show "Pleasure Time" sponsored by Chesterfield.

Chesterfield's own
PATSY GARRETT
of Fred Waring's "Pleasure Time"
with PAT O'BRIEN
America's popular screen star

Chesterfield

NARRAGANSETT BREWING COMPANY • CRANSTON • RHODE ISLAND

Narragansett Brewing Company of Rhode Island was one of the most popular regional breweries. Many advertising agencies pitched for their business. This ad, which ran during 1941, was illustrated by Dr. Seuss, who would in future years achieve great fame.

KEEP U. S. A. OUT OF WAR

Your Part in Keeping the U. S. A. Free of War and Dictatorship

Write today to both of your Senators (Massachusetts Senators are David I. Walsh and Henry Cabot Lodge, Jr.). Address them at the Senate Office Building, Washington, D. C. Ask them to oppose Bill No. 1776, the Bill of Wrongs which would nullify the Bill of Rights, "a bill to authorize undeclared war in the name of Peace and dictatorship in the name of Defending Democracy."

The President would have absolute power, if this Bill is passed, to do the following without consulting Congress or the people: Cancel the Neutrality Act; Send our warships and merchant vessels and possible to manufacture an incident in the east as well as the west almost the world over and leave our home shores weak and defenseless.

NOW IS THE TIME TO ACT—Write yourself, simply, clearly—telephone your friends to do the same. Get telegrams in as well but most important, write in person.

Peace House, working with religious and peace organizations of long standing, appeals to all young men who are opposed to war from either religious or humanitarian convictions to register

"CONSCIENTIOUS OBJECTOR"

on their draft questionnaire. After years of ardent work for peace our Government recognizes this right. Do not allow the opportunity to escape.

It is a matter of interest to observe that after England's many months of war, Canada does not have compulsory military service for overseas and has no Lease-Lend Bill but is SELLING armaments in large quantities to her mother country. In England over 50,000 Conscientious Objectors are helping their government in peaceful employment.

May not our own beloved country be also accused of war mongering while arming England through the front door and simultaneously slipping munitions to Germany through Russia?

The war in Africa, etc., has certainly no conceivable attribute of democracy. Gandhi, called the only heroic figure of the 20th century, expressed himself recently as follows: "It is a matter of deep regret to me that the Government (British) have not been able to appreciate the Congress (Indian) position—who felt a conscientious objection to helping a war which they regard—as one for saving imperialism, of which India is the greatest victim."

To the Clergy: The undersigned wishes to respectfully entreat you to draw the attention of your congregation to the Ten Commandments as a mode of life to be exercised in the relations between nations as well as individuals.

For further information if you are convinced that the killing of your fellow man is contrary to the law of God and man write, enclosing a carefully, self-addressed stamped envelope. Address your letter to

Mrs. J. Sergeant Cram

PEACE HOUSE

110th St. and Fifth Ave., N. Y. City
Inquire about Peace Prizes
ESTABLISHED 1923

This was one of the many advertisements which were scheduled in most major daily newspapers advocating the U.S.A. stay out of the raging European war.

FEAR

HEAR

THE FRESHER THE BREAD
THE BETTER THE TOAST
GET WONDER BREAD FRESH
AND THEN HEAR HIM BOAST

DEAR

How To Simply, Quickly Prove
Fresh Wonder Bread Toasts Better

**Make The 60-Second Test
Against Your Present Bread
—In Your Own Toaster**

I LOVE THIS FRESH WONDER BREAD!

IT'S SLO-BAKED
WONDER BREAD

... SLO-BAKED
FOR LASTING FRESHNESS

DISCOVER now for yourself the toast fresh Wonder Bread makes—in this 60-second test: a slice of Wonder Bread, a slice of your present bread toasted at the same time . . . for the same time . . . in your toaster.

Note how fresh Wonder Bread comes out browned gold all over . . . with crust delicately crisp . . . inside white and lacy and delicate as angel food . . . toast to make your mouth water. You decide which has the better flavor.

Prove to yourself toast made from fresh Wonder Bread tastes better. In impartial bread comparisons made by over 600,000 women in their food stores throughout the country, Wonder Bread was chosen the "one best bread" 9 to 1 for fresh-baked flavor, fresh soft texture and oven-fresh aroma. Try fresh Wonder Bread for sandwiches, too.

REMEMBER—NOTHING BUT THE BEST IS GOOD ENOUGH FOR YOUR FAMILY —GET FRESH WONDER BREAD TODAY IN THE RED, YELLOW AND BLUE BALLOON WRAPPER

Continental Baking Co., Inc.

Here's an ad loaded with many diversified reasons why you should serve your family Wonder Bread. The body copy included reference to an impartial bread comparison. "Over 600,000 women in their food stores throughout the country. Wonder Bread was chosen the one best bread 9 to 1 for fresh-baked flavor, fresh soft texture and oven-fresh aroma." Would this statement be acceptable today? Would the media ask for proof or more specifics on how the survey was taken? Possibly.

"That's A H--l of a Way to Run a Railroad!"

This ad, created in 1948 by Harold Cabot, offered many reasons why families and workers should make use of Boston and Maine trains during the winter season. The headline was daring and apologies were offered for being frank.

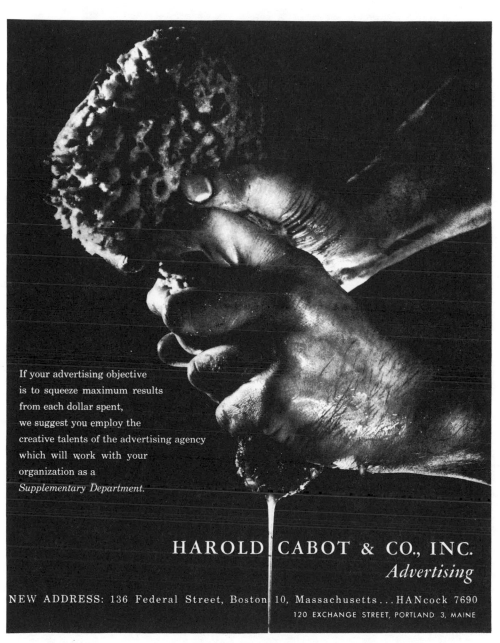

If your advertising objective
is to squeeze maximum results
from each dollar spent,
we suggest you employ the
creative talents of the advertising agency
which will work with your
organization as a
Supplementary Department.

HAROLD CABOT & CO., INC.
Advertising

NEW ADDRESS: 136 Federal Street, Boston 10, Massachusetts...HANcock 7690
120 EXCHANGE STREET, PORTLAND 3, MAINE

In 1949, Harold Cabot & Co., Inc., ran this self-promoting
ad in Boston newspapers to attract new clients.

During the winter of 1948-49, the Harold Cabot advertising agency of Boston created a series of newspaper ads for the Boston and Maine Railroad urging motorists to take it easy and take the train. Decades later, Boston's MBTA would also launch an advertising campaign to urge commuters to use the MBTA.

Index